Christopher Columbus

A LATTER-DAY SAINT PERSPECTIVE

RELIGIOUS STUDIES CENTER PUBLICATIONS

BOOK OF MORMON SYMPOSIUM SERIES

The Book of Mormon: The Keystone Scripture
The Book of Mormon: First Nephi, the Doctrinal Foundation
The Book of Mormon: Second Nephi, the Doctrinal Structure
The Book of Mormon: Jacob Through Words of Mormon, To Learn with Joy
The Book of Mormon: Mosiah, Salvation Only Through Christ
The Book of Mormon: Alma, The Testimony of the Word

MONOGRAPH SERIES

Nibley on the Timely and the Timeless
Deity and Death
The Glory of God Is Intelligence
Reflections on Mormonism
Literature of Belief
The Words of Joseph Smith
Book of Mormon Authorship
Mormons and Muslims
The Temple in Antiquity
Isaiah and the Prophets
Scriptures for the Modern World
The Joseph Smith Translation: The Restoration of Plain and Precious Things
Apocryphal Writings and the Latter-day Saints
The Pearl of Great Price: Revelations From God
The Lectures on Faith in Historical Perspective

SPECIALIZED MONOGRAPH SERIES

Supporting Saints: Life Stories of Nineteenth-Century Mormons
The Call of Zion: The Story of the First Welsh Mormon Emigration
The Religion and Family Connection: Social Science Perspectives
Welsh Mormon Writings from 1844 to 1862: A Historical Bibliography
Peter and the Popes
John Lyon: The Life of a Pioneer Poet
Latter-day Prophets and the United States Constitution

OCCASIONAL PAPERS SERIES

Excavations at Seila, Egypt

Christopher Columbus

A LATTER-DAY SAINT PERSPECTIVE

ARNOLD K. GARR

With a Foreword by DeLAMAR JENSEN

Religious Studies Center
Brigham Young University
Provo, Utah

Library of Congress Catalog Card Number: 92–64107
ISBN 0–88494–842–0

First Printing, 1992

Distributed by BOOKCRAFT, INC.
Salt Lake City, Utah

Printed in the United States of America

Contents

	Foreword	ix
	Preface	xiii
1	Columbus: Fulfillment of Book of Mormon Prophecy	1
2	Early Life in Genoa	7
3	Years in Portugal: Emergence of the Grand Idea	19
4	Years in Spain: Columbus Finds a Sponsor	29
5	First Voyage to the Americas: Columbus Guided by the Spirit	39
6	Later Voyages: Columbus as Governor	53
7	Later Years: The Book of Prophecies and the Final Voyage	63
	Epilogue	71
	Appendix A: Statements by Modern-Day Prophets and Apostles on Columbus	73
	Appendix B: Statements by Columbus with Spiritual Significance	81
	Appendix C: One Hundred Eminent Men Baptized by Proxy in the St. George Temple, 21 August 1877	85
	Appendix D: Chronology of Christopher Columbus' Life	87
	Bibliography	93
	Index	99

Foreword

In 1939 Charles Nowell observed in a brief book on the Age of Discovery, that Columbus is "alternately praised and belittled, groomed for canonization and charged with piracy, lauded as a scientist and branded as an ignoramus." Little has changed in the ensuing 53 years, except that the negative evaluations have increased in both frequency and intensity. Why has it become so popular to excoriate a person who was once lauded as the most courageous, energetic, patient, pious, and persevering man ever born?

I suspect that part of the answer lies in the fact that human nature seems to delight in taking pot shots at anyone on a pedestal. Lesser figures can usually slip by unscathed, but people of prominence are always the targets of self-styled critics who find it easier to criticize than to analyze. The temptation is even greater when it is perceived that the subject under scrutiny is more exalted than seems appropriate. There is no doubt that Columbus was mythologized out of proportion in the late eighteenth and early nineteenth centuries by writers such as William Robertson, Charles Goodrich, and especially Washington Irving. Although well-meaning, these three succeeded in creating a mythical Columbus, a greater-than-life sized hero, who had all of the virtues and none of the vices of other mortals. This is the legendary figure whom Americans came to associate with the name Columbus, a man who always saw matters more clearly than anyone else, who alone thought the world was a sphere, against the contrary opinion of the most learned minds of Portugal and Spain, and who made no errors in his geographical and navigational decisions. Had it not been for his illicit love affair with Beatriz Enriquez de Arana, the Admiral would have been canonized in the 1880s.

It is not surprising that scholars have had problems with this nineteenth-century Columbus. He did in fact make many mistakes about geography and navigation. He was in error about the size of the earth, believing it to be much smaller than the majority of his contemporaries thought it was (they were right); and he grossly miscalculated the oceanic distance between the Canary Islands and Japan (Columbus–2400 miles—actual 10,600 miles).

The legitimate debunking of Columbus myths, however, has led to the invention of many new myths, some of which are more flagrant distortions of the truth and certainly more dangerous than the former ones. One of these is that reliable documents and information about Columbus are unavailable and therefore all we can do is conjecture, or fantasize. The fact is, there are a good many authentic and reliable documentary sources on Columbus' life and thought. We don't know everything about the man. There are many gaps, of course, and there are unsolved mysteries, but by and large there is about as much concrete data on Columbus as on any historical figure of 500 years ago, and a good deal more than on most of those who came from such an obscure background without formal education or social advantage. The problem with those who say Columbus is unknowable is that they do not use the sources readily available. They prefer their own conjectures to the drudgery of historical research.

Other, more pernicious, myths have resulted from the marriage of ignorance and perverted political agitation. Thus Columbus has been made the scapegoat for all kinds of contemporary causes, from being responsible for our present environmental pollution to being the evil force behind the exploitation and extermination of millions of native Americans. What these recriminations fail to take into account is that Columbus was not any more oblivious to the environment than were the rest of his contemporaries, or of those who preceded him, on either side of the Atlantic. Neither pollution, cruelty, slavery, nor social injustice began in 1492. These were all flourishing long before Columbus came on the scene.

The present study by Professor Arnold K. Garr does not address these or a great many other issues that confront both Columbus bashers and backers. It is not a polemical work trying to grind a particular political or social ax. Neither does it pause to argue the pros and cons of any number of issues that have been aroused in recent writings, nor go off on a tangent in pursuit of alternative interpretations of Columbus' birth, nationality, or financial motives. It is, however, a book with a point of view. That point of view is Latter-day Saint, unapologetic and undogmatic, characterizing Columbus as both a human being, with human feelings and flaws, and a man of God, with vision, conviction, and a pious devotion to the divine will. Columbus' understanding of that divine will was limited by human frailties, yet he had enduring faith in God's justice and mercy. Columbus believed further that he was divinely called to be an instrument in God's hands to Christianize the islands of the ocean sea and to help redeem Jerusalem prior to the Second Coming of the Savior. All of this Professor Garr treats within the framework of the Book of Mormon prophecies as highlighted in modern ecclesiastical statements. It is a brief but sound study, relying on the best contemporary scholarship and a careful reading of both secular and religious sources.

De Lamar Jensen
Professor Emeritus of History and
Chairman of the Columbus Quincentennial Committee
Brigham Young University

Preface

The world is commemorating the 500th anniversary of Christopher Columbus' first voyage to America. Without question, this voyage is one of the most significant events in the history of humanity. Columbus' expedition brought two worlds into permanent contact with each other, the Old World of Europe and Asia and the "New World" of the Americas, and set in motion a chain of events that would transform both worlds forever. Among other things, Columbus' encounter with the Americas opened the door to a flood of exploration, colonization, missionary work, and fortune-seeking, the likes of which this earth has seldom, if ever, experienced.

As part of this celebration, many books have appeared which analyze the life and achievements of Columbus. Why then another book? While most of the books published thus far have assessed the achievements of Columbus from a secular basis, I have endeavored in this book to look at and discuss his contributions in a spiritual context. This concise overview of Columbus' life is intended primarily for Latter-day Saint readers—people who believe in the Book of Mormon and the teachings of modern-day apostles and prophets.

I have been impressed with and have emphasized seven important themes relative to Columbus' life and accomplishments: (1) his discovery of the Western World was the fulfillment of Book of Mormon Prophecy; (2) he was a forerunner to the restoration of the Gospel of Jesus Christ in these latter days; (3) his prime motive for exploration was to spread Christianity throughout the world; (4) he was guided by the Spirit of God, especially on his first voyage; (5) he, himself, believed he was guided by the Spirit; (6) he believed many of his achievements were a fulfillment of prophecy; and (7) many Latter-day Saint apostles and prophets have held and do hold Columbus in high regard.

As I have prepared this work, I have come to feel a special kinship with Columbus and also with others who have written about him: Samuel Eliot Morison, author of the Pulitzer Prize winning book, *Admiral of the Ocean Sea*; Ferdinand Columbus, the Admiral's son, whose biography of his father, *The Life of the Admiral Christopher Columbus*, while somewhat less critical than one might wish certainly offers many insights into the man Christopher Columbus; Oliver Dunn and James Kelley, Jr., who published *The Diario of Christopher Columbus's First Voyage to America, 1492-1493*, an excellent English translation of the abstract of Columbus' journal of his first trans-Atlantic expedition; and finally, Delno C. West and August Kling, whose *The Libro de las Profecias of Christopher Columbus* is an outstanding English translation of and commentary on Columbus' *Book of Prophecies*. I have relied heavily upon these works and am indebted to these authors.

I am also very grateful to many people who helped me with this present project: Robert L. Millet, Dean of Religious Education and General Director of the Religious Studies Center at Brigham Young University, who encouraged me to publish this work and provided a research grant to make it possible; Leon R. Hartshorn, chair of the Department of Church History and Doctrine at BYU, who graciously rearranged my teaching schedule so I could have the time necessary to complete this study; and Charles D. Tate, Jr., Assistant General Director—Publications of the Religious Studies Center, Charlotte Pollard and Curtis Bay of his staff, who have provided expert, professional editing for this work. To Richard O. Cowan, my good friend and mentor, and De Lamar Jensen, a distinguished historian and chairman of BYU's Columbus Quincentennial Committee, go my thanks for reading the manuscript and offering many helpful suggestions, and to Dr. Jensen for writing the Foreword.

My research assistant, Fred Williams, and secretary, Mary Kay Robinson, have also helped make it possible for me to meet the deadlines for this manuscript.

I would especially like to thank my wife, Cherie, and our children, Wendi, Natalie, Randy, Rob, and Cory, for their kind understanding when I had to be working on this project rather than doing something with them. Finally, I would like to express appreciation to my mother, Lucile Garr, for her many years of love and encouragement.

CHAPTER ONE

Columbus: Fulfillment of Book of Mormon Prophecy

And I looked and beheld a man among the Gentiles, who was separated from the seed of my brethren by the many waters; and I beheld the Spirit of God, that it came down and wrought upon the man; and he went forth upon the many waters, even unto the seed of my brethren, who were in the promised land.

—1 Nephi 13:12

For Latter-day Saints, the story of Christopher Columbus begins long before he was born in 1451. In fact, what he would do was known in prophecy at least 600 years before the birth of Christ, when the ancient American prophet, Nephi, foresaw Columbus' coming to the New World in a vision and recorded what he saw on metal plates. Joseph Smith later translated that account as part of the Book of Mormon. The record of the vision is found in the 1 Nephi 13:12. Nephi declared: "I looked and beheld a man among the Gentiles, who was separated from the seed of my brethren by the many waters; and I beheld the Spirit of God, that it came down and wrought upon the man; and he went forth upon the many waters, even unto the seed of my brethren, who were in the promised land."

Elder Mark E. Petersen, a modern-day apostle, explained that "the many waters were the Atlantic Ocean," and that "the seed of [Nephi's] brethren were the American Indians." He also affirmed that "it was Christopher Columbus whom [Nephi] saw, and he observed further that the discoverer was guided by divine power on his journey" (Petersen 3).

Several modern-day prophets have testified that Columbus was guided to the New World by the Spirit of God , fulfilling Book of Mormon prophecy. In 1976, President Ezra Taft Benson stated, "God inspired 'a man among the Gentiles' . . . who, by the Spirit of God was led to rediscover the land of America and bring this rich new land to the attention of the people in Europe. That man, of course, was Christopher Columbus, who testified that he was inspired in what he did" (Benson 577).

In 1950, Elder Spencer W. Kimball testified that God "inspired a little boy, Christopher Columbus, to stand on the quays in Genoa, Italy, and yearn for the sea. He was filled with the desire to sail the seas, and he fulfilled a great prophecy made long, long ago that this land, chosen above all other lands, should be discovered. And so when he was mature, opportunity was granted to him to brave the unknown seas, to find this land . . . and to open the door, as it were" (Kimball 427).

In 1907, President Joseph F. Smith also confirmed his conviction that the Lord guided Columbus in much the same way as He did Adam and Abraham in the Old Testament (Smith, Joseph F. 31).

Church leaders' statements about Columbus are not restricted to those of the 20th Century, as the apostles and prophets from the beginning of this dispensation also boldly testified that the Lord guided the great discoverer. In 1869, Elder George Q. Cannon delivered an address in the Salt Lake Tabernacle in which he stated: "Columbus was inspired to penetrate the ocean and discover this Western continent, for the set time for its discovery had come; and the consequences which God desired to follow its discovery have taken place" (*Journal of Discourses* 14:55; hereafter *JD*).

At the 1854 Fourth of July celebration in Salt Lake City, President Brigham Young spoke of the Lord's direction of the events that led to the modern discovery of America: "The Almighty . . . moved upon Columbus to launch forth upon the trackless deep to discover the American Continent" (*JD* 7:13). Elder Orson Hyde, speaking at the same celebration as President Young, made perhaps the most intriguing reference to this theme, connecting Columbus' voyage and discoveries with the ministry of Moroni, the ancient American prophet and divine messenger and caretaker of the records of the Book of Mormon. Referring to him as the "Prince of America," Elder Hyde noted that Moroni "presides over the destinies of America, and feels a lively interest in all our doings. . . . This same angel was with Columbus and gave him deep impressions, by dreams and by visions, respecting this New World." He continued, "The angel of God helped him—was with him on the stormy deep, calmed the troubled elements, and guided his frail vessel to the desired haven" (*JD* 6:368). It is abundantly clear from these and other statements that Church leaders from early on have taught that the Lord was very interested in the success of Columbus' voyages to and from the Americas.

Columbus left many statements in his journals and other personal writings in which he boldly declare that he believed the Lord directed him in his great undertaking. Referring to his first voyage to America, he once stated, "With a hand that could be felt, the Lord opened my mind to the fact that it would be possible to sail from here to the Indies. . . . This was the fire that burned within me. . . . Who can doubt that this fire was not merely mine, but also of the Holy Spirit" (West and Kling 105; Columbus most often referred to the New World as the Indies).

Forerunner to the Restoration of the Gospel

One might ask why the Lord was so concerned with Columbus that He guided the discoverer in his preparation for the journey and inspired him along the way. The answer to this question can also be found in the writings of modern-day apostles and prophets. Several have clearly stated that Columbus and also the Founding Fathers of the United States of America were instruments in the Lord's hands in preparing America to become the seat of the Restoration of the Gospel of Jesus Christ in this last dispensation of time.

In 1903, President Joseph F. Smith spoke of the divine destiny of America: "This great American nation the Almighty raised up by the power of his omnipotent hand, that it might be possible in the latter days for the kingdom of God to be established in the earth." President Smith further explained that, "if the Lord had not prepared the way by laying the foundations of this glorious nation, it would have been impossible (under the stringent laws and bigotry of the monarchical governments of the world) to have laid the foundation of the coming of his great kingdom. The Lord has done this" (Smith, Joseph F. 409).

Echoing this same idea, Elder Mark E. Petersen said: "The true gospel . . . could not be given to Israel of today until it was restored, and the restoration could come only under favorable conditions, in a free country, where men could worship God according to the dictates of their own conscience" (Petersen 4). Speaking specifically about the work that Columbus and the Founding Fathers performed, Elder Petersen declared: "These events were preliminary steps leading up to the gospel being restored and taken to the entire house of Israel." He emphasized that, "few people think of the discovery of America, the Revolutionary War, and the establishment of a constitutional form of government here as being steps toward the fulfillment of the Lord's ancient covenant with Abraham. *But it is a fact that they were*" (Ibid. 3; emphasis added).

Finally, George Q. Cannon specifically named Columbus, along with George Washington, Thomas Jefferson, John Adams and Benjamin Franklin as men who "were inspired to do the work they did." He declared that, "it was a preparatory work for the establishment of the kingdom of God. This Church and kingdom could not have been established on the earth if their work had not been performed" (*JD* 14:55).

Latter-day Saints conclude that the Lord inspired Columbus to be a forerunner in preparing the way for the establishment of the kingdom of God on the American continent in this last dispensation. As Elder Petersen explained, "The restoration of the gospel of the Lord Jesus Christ in these latter days, together with the advance preparation of conditions which made it possible, was indeed a divine drama which had many stages and many scenes, some of which were world shaking" (Petersen 2). Let us now turn our attention to the life of a man who truly changed the world as he played out his part in this divine drama. That man, of course, is Christopher Columbus, and the scene is the Age of Discovery.

CHAPTER TWO

Early Life in Genoa

I am sure that [God] inspired a little boy, Christopher Columbus, to stand on the quays of Genoa, Italy, and yearn for the sea.

—President Spencer W. Kimball

When he was about 50 years old, Christopher Columbus wrote a letter to the Spanish monarchs, Ferdinand and Isabella, which contained the following brief sketch of his youth and preparation for life: "At a very early age I began to navigate upon the seas, which I have continued to this day. . . . Such has been my interest for more than forty years. . . . I prayed to the most merciful Lord concerning my desire, and he gave me the spirit and the intelligence for it" (West and Kling 105). Other than this, Columbus wrote very little about his youth in his personal writings; consequently he left to his biographers the task of piecing together the events of his early years. Fortunately, several historians have done admirable work.

When was Columbus born? The exact date of Columbus' birth is not known because no records have ever been found. However, there are two documents which narrow the possible date of his birth to sometime between 25 August and 31 October, probably in the year 1451. The first document was a deposition dated 31 October 1470 wherein Christopher stated that he was over nineteen years of age. The second is called the

Asserto Document of 25 August 1479, in which he declared that he was twenty-seven years old or thereabouts. If he was older than nineteen and not yet twenty on 31 October 1470, and about twenty-seven on 25 August 1479, Columbus was most likely born between 25 August and the end of October, 1451 (Morison, *Admiral*, 1:10, 23n17; hereafter noted by author and volume: page).

Inasmuch as Columbus became such a famous world figure, writers from many nations have tried to claim him as a native son. Even though all of the reputable historians of his day maintained that he was born in the Italian Republic of Genoa, several authors in the past two centuries have challenged that fact. Motivated primarily by fanatic nationalism, various historians have claimed he was born in such diverse places as Castile, Portugal, France, Germany, England, and even Greece. Still, others have tried to prove he was a Jew of Spanish descent (Morison 1:7–9). The most respected scholars of our day, however, have produced documents that support the original premise that he was born in Genoa. The most important record is a *majorat* or *entail* of his estate that he executed on 22 February 1498. In it, he charged his heirs "always to work for the honor, welfare and increase of the city of Genoa." A house would be maintained in that city for some member of their family, "so that he can live there honorably and have foot and root in that city as a native thereof . . . *because from it I came and in it I was born.*" Noting "*Being as I was born in Genoa,*" Columbus directed the executors to accumulate a fund in the bank of St. George at Genoa, that "noble and powerful city by the sea" (Morison 1:7; emphasis added; see also Taviani, *The Grand Design*, 15–46, 223–70).

Religious Significance of the Name

Like so many other aspects of his life, even the story behind Columbus' name carries a certain amount of mystique. His name in Italian was Cristoforo Columbo, by which he was known until he was an adult. After he moved to Spain, however, his name became the Spanish Cristóbal Colón, by which he is known throughout the Spanish speaking world. English speakers, of course, refer to him as Christopher Columbus, thereby Anglicizing his first name and using the Latin version of his surname.

Christopher's son, Ferdinand, believed that God directed the choice of his father's names. For example, the name Christopher means Christ-bearer. St. Christopher, according to legend, received that name because he carried the Christ-child across a deep river at the peril of his own life. Because of this heroic deed, he became known as the patron saint of travelers. Just as St. Christopher carried the Savior across treacherous waters, Ferdinand reasoned that his father risked his life to carry the message of Christ across the dangerous waters of the Atlantic to the heathens of the New World (Ferdinand Columbus, *Life of the Admiral Christopher Columbus* 4-5; cited hereafter as Ferdinand to distinguish him from his father).

The *Columbus* surname was common in Southern Europe, and means "dove." Ferdinand also believed that this name was providential because his father, "carried the grace of the Holy Ghost to that New World . . . showing those people . . . God's beloved son, as the Holy Ghost did in the figure of the dove when St. John baptized Christ" (Ferdinand 4). The religious symbolism of his name does seem significant, considering the Admiral's professed faith and the inspiration to which he attributed his great success.

Perhaps the most intriguing aspect of Columbus' name, however, is the way in which he signed it after he returned home from his first voyage to the New World. Although there were several variations, the most common rendering was as follows:

.S.
.S.A.S.
X M Y
Xpo FERENS

The most complete explanation of this curious cryptic autograph by Columbus himself is, at best, vague. In his will, he simply instructed his heirs on the mechanics, spacing, and punctuation of the signature. Though he left no clues as to its meaning, he directed them to use the cryptic signature, thereafter, as their own (Thacher 3:455; this volume has 371 pages on Columbus' handwriting). Scholars generally agree that the signature denotes some kind of tribute to Christianity. On the bottom line, $X\overline{po}$ is Greek for "Christ," and FERENS is Latin meaning "bearer." Many interpretations suggest that the X M Y, one line above, stand for "O Christ, Mary, Joseph!" The top four letters of the pyramid may stand for either, "Save me" or, "I am the servant of the Most High Saviour." According to Thacher (3:456–57), the complete message might well be:

I am the servant of the Most High Saviour
O Christ, Mary, Joseph!
Christ-bearer

Bedini lists several other possible interpretations of the signature (Bedini 628–30). But if Thacher's interpretation is correct, Columbus was far from being timid in declaring his faith in Christ and his divine calling, as he employed variations of this signature in at least 33 existing documents signed after the first voyage (Thacher 3:454). Historians generally agree that Columbus used the signature on most important documents for the rest of his life.

Childhood in Genoa: the Making of a Man

With that, let us now leave the story of Columbus' name and give consideration to his early life. Christopher was the oldest of five children born to Domenico Columbo and Susanna Fontanarossa. He had three brothers: Giovanni Pellegrino, who died when he was a young man; Bartholomew, who helped Columbus plan his Enterprise of the Indies; and Giacomo, better known as Diego (the Spanish equivalent), whom the Admiral took with him on his second voyage to the New World. Christopher only had one sister, Bianchinetta, about whom we know very little.

Christopher's father, Domenico, was a master weaver and merchant. On one or more occasions, when his local political party was in power, he was also appointed keeper of the Olivella Gate on Genoa's east side. This position paid 84 Genoese pounds a year (or about $160 in gold) from which he was expected to pay his assistants. Inasmuch as Domenico was a master clothier (not just a journeyman weaver) and sometimes the recipient of political patronage, we may assume that he was a respected artisan and businessman of the lower middle class (Morison 1:12–14).

We know that, as an adult, Christopher could read and write, but historians disagree about where he attended school, if he did at all, and the extent of his early education. Ferdinand Columbus unequivocally declared that his father, "learned his letters at a tender age and studied enough at the University of Pavia to understand the geographers, of whose teaching he was very fond" (Ferdinand 9). However, Professor Morison maintained that the well-preserved records of Pavia University do not support Ferdinand's claim (Morison 1:17–18). Dr. Aldo Agosto, director of the provincial archives of Genoa, speculated that Columbus might have been enrolled in a monastery school near Genoa called Paverano, whose name Ferdinand may have confused with "Pavia" (Lyon 12). Others have suggested that Columbus attended a school run by the wool guild of Genoa on Pavia Street (Nader 1:164).

Whatever the truth may be about the location and timing of his early education, we know that by the time Columbus settled in Spain, at age 33, he could read and write Spanish. Even the letters that he sent to business acquaintances and friends in Genoa were written in Spanish. Morison went so far as to propose that Spanish was the language of Columbus' thoughts. The Admiral's written Spanish was littered with Portuguese spellings, a reminder of a decade spent sailing from Portugal before he finally moved to Spain. In addition, he was able to read Latin and to speak Genoese, an unwritten dialect which differed greatly from Italian. Incidentally, there is no compelling evidence that he ever learned to read or write Italian (Morison 1:18–19).

We have no physical descriptions of Columbus in his youth, but several contemporaries who knew him personally as an adult have left some very helpful verbal portraits of him. Oviedo, the official chronicler of "the Indies," who witnessed the Admiral's triumphant entry into Barcelona after his first voyage to America, described him as "taller than the average and strongly limbed: the eyes lively and other parts of the face of good proportion, the hair very red, and the face somewhat ruddy and freckled" (Morison 1:62). Morison quoted Bartolomé de las Casas as saying, "He was more than middling tall; face long and giving an air of authority; aquiline nose, blue eyes, complexion light and tending to bright red; beard and hair red when young but very soon turned gray from his labors" (Ibid 62–63).

His contemporaries also gave a brief glimpse at Columbus' personality and character. Oviedo claimed he was "fair in speech, tactful and of great creative talent; a nice Latinist and most learned cosmographer; gracious when he wished to be, irascible when annoyed" (Morison 1:62). Ferdinand maintained that his father, "was so great an enemy to cursing and swearing" that he "never heard him utter any other oath than by 'St. Ferdinand!'" (Ferdinand 9).

It is also vitally important that we understand Columbus' attitude toward religion. We are indebted to the great priest-historian, Las Casas, and others, for a brief description of the Admiral's religiosity: "In matters of the Christian religion, without doubt he was a Catholic and of great devotion. . . . He observed the fasts of the Church most faithfully, confessed and made communion often, read the canonical offices like a churchman or member of a religious order, hated blasphemy and profane swearing" (Morison 1:63). The priest further pointed to Columbus' belief in divine blessings: "he hourly admitted that God had conferred upon him great mercies, as upon David. When gold or precious things were brought to him, he entered his cabin, knelt down, summoned the bystanders, and said, 'Let us give thanks to Our Lord'" (Ibid).

Las Casas also revealed the Admiral's fervent desire to carry the message of Christ to the world: "He was extraordinarily zealous for the divine service; he desired and was eager for the conversion of these people [the Indians], and that in every region the faith of Jesus Christ be planted and enhanced . . . ever holding great confidence in divine providence" (Morison 1:63–64). From this statement, as well as from others we will later discuss, we see that the Admiral's prime motivation for sailing across the ocean was to help spread Christianity throughout the earth.

The World of Columbus

In the mid-fifteenth century, when Christopher Columbus was growing up, two important events occurred that significantly altered the political, economic, and cultural structure of Europe, and also had a great impact on Columbus. First, the Ottoman Empire attacked and captured Constantinople in 1453. The siege lasted six weeks and is regarded by many historians as one of the most dramatic events in world history. Constantinople had been a Christian stronghold, and its fall to the Muslims signaled a major defeat for Christianity.

European merchants had even greater concern about the loss of the city. From Constantinople, the Turks began to expand into the Aegean and Adriatic Seas, and eventually took the Italian port of Otranto in 1480. This rapid expansion of a force hostile to Genoa's mercantile designs altered the course of activities of her sea-faring merchants. Whereas the Genoese had traditionally traded in the profitable spice and aromatics markets of the eastern Mediterranean, the Ottoman expansion severely restricted Genoese access to these markets and sources of merchandise. By 1475, the Ottomans had captured Caffa,

Genoa's sole remaining trading post in the Black Sea. They eventually conquered Syria, Palestine, and much of Africa, and by the 1520's, controlled parts of Central Europe. Historians suggest that the Ottoman Empire's threat to Genoese autonomy was so great that only an internal power struggle within the Empire in 1481 prevented it from having an even greater effect on the history of Europe, and especially on Renaissance Italy (McKay, Hill, and Buckler 724).

In short, the Ottoman aggression in the eastern Mediterranean significantly restricted European sea expeditions. It should not surprise anyone that Columbus began to visualize a western course to the Indies: such a route would give access to the very profitable eastern markets without having to cross Ottoman territory.

The second development in fifteenth-century Europe which affected Columbus and the rest of the world forever was the invention of the printing press around 1455. Johann Gutenberg, probably with the help of Johann Fust and Peter Schöffer, made the breakthrough that would aid in making books much less expensive to have. By the mid-1400's, paper was widely available in Europe, and printing stimulated the literacy among lay people and, in turn, deeply affected their private lives (McKay, Hill, and Buckler 506). The Gutenberg Bible was printed in 1456, and many other texts appeared soon after.

The invention of the printing press was a key to promoting individual freedom and thought, paving the way for religious freedom and promoting the faith and devotion of lay people like Columbus. With a Bible of his own, Christopher now had instant access to the scriptures, and his personal study of them increased the influence of the Holy Ghost in his life. With this new-found source of freedom and independence in place, it is no wonder that other events which changed the course of history began to take place, including the beginning of the Protestant Reformation only 25 years after Columbus' first voyage.

Early Years at Sea

The fact that Christopher Columbus was an accomplished and skillful sailor is well documented. The beginnings of his affair with the sea, however, are not so clear. Still, historians generally agree that his exposure to the maritime world began at an early age. Situated conveniently between surrounding hills and the shore, Genoa had a bustling harbor that was the area's center of attention.

It is likely that Christopher spent a good part of his childhood in and about the port of Genoa, watching ships arrive and set sail again. Because of its deep and protected harbor and its position on the major highway from Italy to France, Genoa had one of the busiest seaports in Europe (Nader 1:167). City workers built and expanded the harbor, dock workers loaded and unloaded cargoes, and the city's shipyards turned out the newest designs in sailing vessels year after year. In the midst of such a flurry of activity, young Christopher probably gained his first view of the seafarer's life and began sailing before adulthood. In fact, Antonio Gallo, a Genoese historian who knew the Columbus family, stated that the Columbus boys began sailing as teenagers (Thacher 1:192–93).

The exact starting date when Christopher began his sailing experience is not known. However, in a 1501 letter to Ferdinand and Isabella, he wrote: "I have passed more than forty years in this business and have traveled to every place where there is navigation up to the present time" (Ferdinand 10). This statement would place his introduction to the sea at around 1461, which would be at about age 10. In another statement to his son Ferdinand, Columbus claimed that he began sailing at age 14, or around 1465 (Ibid 12). In 1492, Christopher wrote in his journal, "I have been at sea 23 years without leaving it for any time worth telling," thus putting the start of his career at age 18 (Dunn and Kelley 253). Columbus' imprecision over when he began his sailing career can be attributed to varying definitions of "going to sea": was he referring to his first experience playing

The World of the Mediterranean

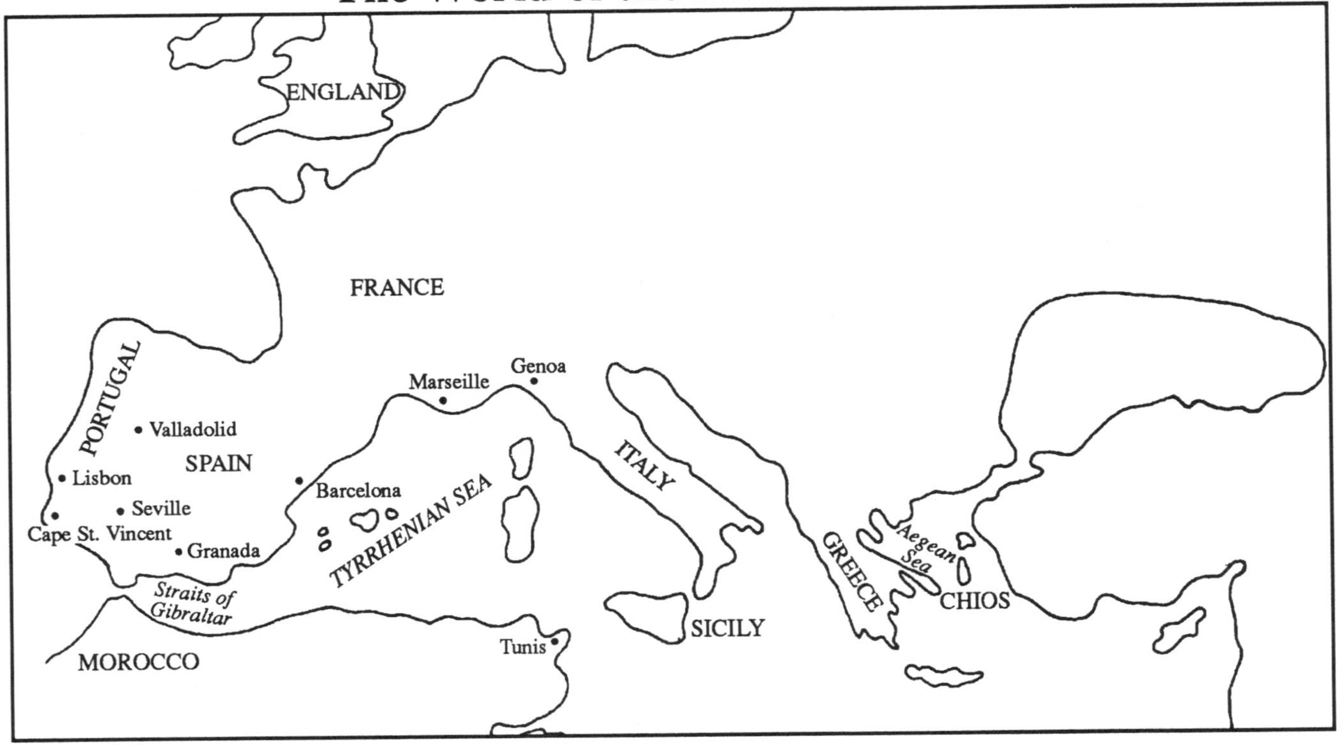

with boats, his first overnight journey, or his first long journey? (Morison 1:27). Whatever the exact date, all are agreed that Columbus went to sea early in life, and he apparently never turned from it.

The evidence that Christopher worked as a sea merchant is substantial. Despite a seventeenth-century French attack on Genoa that destroyed many legal and notarial records, several receipts exist that place Columbus in different ports, participating in trade during the 1470's. Documents show that he traded in wine in Genoa on 31 October 1470, and in wool in Savona on 20 March and 26 August 1472 (Morison 1:26, 29; see also Nader 169–70). Columbus also spoke of an early trip to Tunis and Marseilles in the Mediterranean Sea (Ferdinand 11).

We know that Columbus had sailed to the Genoese trading outpost on Chios in the Aegean Sea because when he attempted to describe many of the native plants he saw on his first voyage to the New World, he likened a tree he saw there to the mastic trees he had "seen on the island of Chios" (Dunn and Kelley 145).

By age 25, Columbus had had substantial experience at sea. Historic documents indicate that he was actively involved in Mediterranean trade in his young adult years. These experiences at sea prepared him for even more significant voyages to come.

CHAPTER THREE

Years In Portugal: Emergence of the Grand Idea

During this time, I have searched out and studied all kinds of texts: geographies, histories, chronologies, philosophies, and other subjects. . . . The Lord opened my mind to the fact that it would be possible to sail from here to the Indies, and he opened my will to desire to accomplish the project.

—Christopher Columbus

A major turning point in Christopher Columbus' life happened when he moved from Genoa to Portugal in 1476. The story of this move is one of adventure, courage and inspiration. It began in May 1476, when he signed on to sail with a Genoese merchant fleet bound for England. The Spinola and DiNegro families sponsored a convoy of five ships to carry goods to Portugal, Flanders, and England. Going on this voyage provided Columbus an opportunity to sail for the first time on the Great Ocean sea, as the Atlantic was then called. The fleet experienced relatively smooth sailing during the early stages of the journey, sailing westward on the Mediterranean through the Strait of Gibraltar, then northward on the spacious Atlantic.

On 13 August, as they were sailing near the coast of Portugal, a French war fleet of at least 13 ships launched a surprise attack against the Genoese convoy. They fought all day, and by nightfall, three Genoese and four French vessels had been sunk, drowning hundreds of men. Columbus' ship caught fire, and the blaze spread so rapidly that the crew was unable to extinguish it. Their only recourse was to jump overboard and cast their fate with the sea. Even though he was as much as six miles off shore, Columbus was able to reach land. Ferdinand says he used the aid of a free-floating oar, but the Phillipses reject that story as being over dramatic and say "we simply do not know" how Columbus made it to shore (Phillips and Phillips 95).

However, Ferdinand believed that the Lord had intervened on this occasion in order to save his father's life, claiming that it "pleased God, who was preserving him for greater things, to give him strength to reach the shore" (Ferdinand 14). This incident was no doubt one of the many times that Columbus was "wrought upon" by the Spirit of God, as foretold in 1 Nephi 13:12. Certainly, it was not time for him to die inasmuch as he had not yet fulfilled his prophesied destiny.

Columbus eventually found his way to Lisbon, Portugal, where he took up residence in a colony of Genoese merchants. He established a map-making business which was his occupation when he was not at sea. It seems, indeed, providential that Christopher would choose to live in Lisbon, because at the time it was the world center for oceanic sailing and discovery. Prince Henry the Navigator, of Portugal, had established an important research center at Cape St. Vincent to study oceanic navigation and to encourage voyages of exploration down the west coast of Africa. In the 1460s and 1470s, the Portuguese continued to inch their way down the African coast in hopes of one day rounding the southern tip of the continent and sailing east to India and Asia. Without a doubt, they were the world's preeminent sailors and explorers in this period of history, and

Columbus' new home was their center for operations (Morison 1:39–41).

Adventures on the Atlantic

In this new environment, Columbus could not resist the lure of the ocean and eventually found himself back at sea, sailing just north of Iceland. He wrote, "In the month of February, 1477, I sailed one hundred leagues beyond the island of Tile [Iceland] . . . which is as big as England. . . . When I was there the sea was not frozen, but the tides were so great that in some places they rose twenty-six fathoms, and fell as much in depth" (Ferdinand 11). With this trip, he had braved the northern ocean, broadened his navigational experience, and possibly even increased his desire to explore further.

In the summer of 1478, the DiNegro family employed Columbus once again, this time to sail to the Madeira Islands to buy 60,000 pounds of sugar for transport to Genoa. On this voyage, he sailed south and west into the Atlantic Ocean, returning to Lisbon after making delivery at Genoa (Fernández-Armesto 29). With the completion of this voyage, the young captain further expanded his oceanic experience and deepened his thirst for adventure.

Christopher and Felipa

The next important step in the life of Columbus was his marriage, probably in 1479, to Felipa Perestrello e Moniz, the daughter of Portuguese nobles. Scholars give particular attention to Christopher's marriage not only for its romance, but also for the impact that it had on the future of his career. Inasmuch as he was a foreigner of relatively low birth who had literally washed ashore just a few years earlier, one might wonder how Christopher was able to marry into a family of noble descent.

Felipa's father, Bartholomew Perestrello, was among the first to colonize the Madeira Islands, and later received the

Seaports of the Atlantic

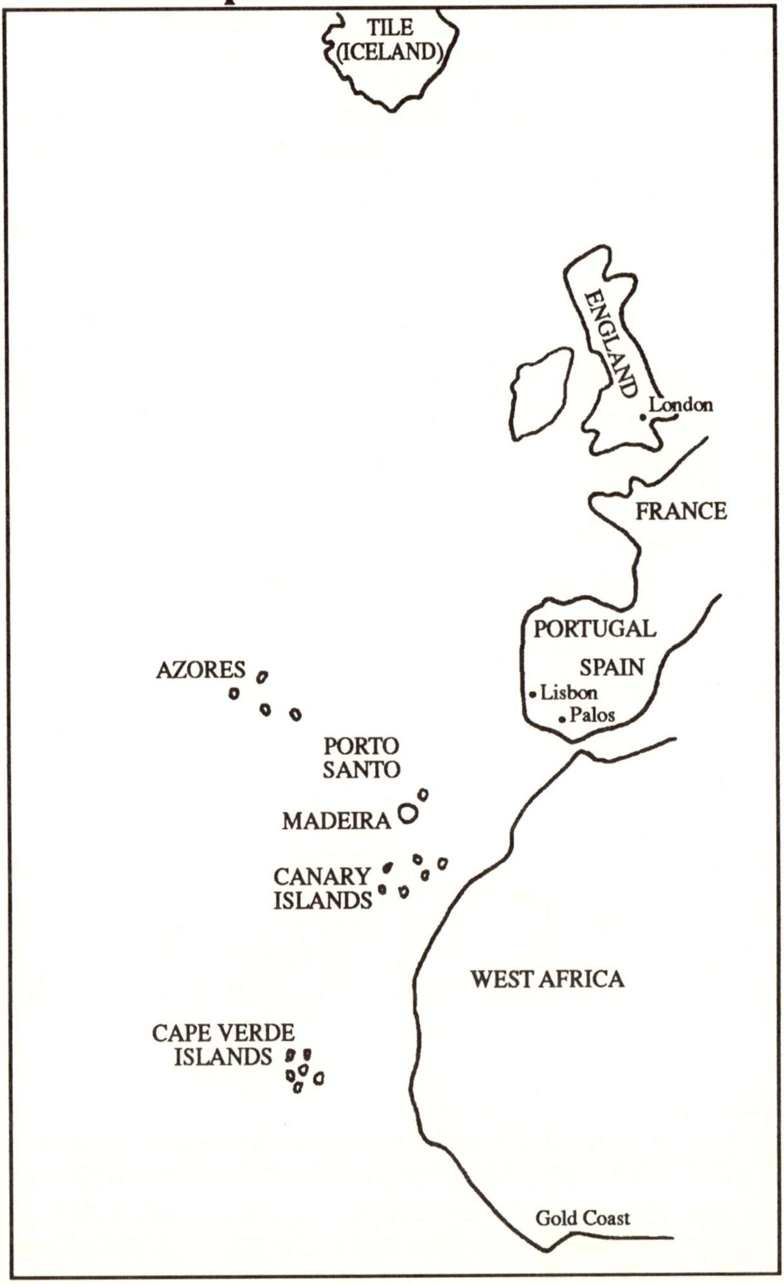

hereditary title of Captain of Porto Santo, an island in the Madeiras. After his death in 1457, his wife, Isabel Moniz, sold her rights to the captaincy of Porto Santo, evidently intending to live off the proceeds of the sale. However, her son, Bartholomew, sued for the return of the rights to him, as the rightful benefactor of the captaincy, leaving his mother with "slender means to support her rank" (Morison 1:50–51).

At this time, Felipa was about 25 years old and was enrolled in the boarding school called Convento dos Santos (Convent of the Saints) near Columbus' map-making establishment. Christopher, being a good Catholic, met Felipa while attending mass in the chapel at the convent (Las Casas 19). The only primary source description we have of their courtship is Ferdinand's. He notes that since Christopher "behaved very honorably and was a man of handsome presence and one who never turned from the path of honesty, . . . [Felipa] had such conversation and friendship with him that she became his wife" (Ferdinand 14). Her mother, Isabel, suffering from the loss of income due to her son's recent suit for the captaincy of Porto Santo, was probably quite pleased to have Felipa married, thereby offering relief from the burden of supporting her.

By marrying Felipa, a daughter of nobility, Columbus effectively gained access to the royal courts of Europe, and eventually was able to sell his adventurous plan to the monarchs of neighboring Spain. Historians seem agreed that had he married a woman of lower status, Columbus probably never would have gained a royal audience to sponsor his expedition.

At first the newlyweds lived with Felipa's widowed mother who, observing Christopher's lively interest in navigation, shared stories of her late husband's seafaring adventures. She also gave Christopher the writings, navigational instruments, and sea-charts that her husband had left behind. This information fired Columbus' imagination so much that he and Felipa soon decided to sail to the Madeiras to live on the islands that her father had helped colonize (Tarvani, *The Great Adventure*, 38–39). The young couple apparently spent most of the next few years living in the Madeiras, both on Porto Santo and in Funchal. This must have been a pleasant time for Columbus. During these years he enjoyed going over his late father-in-law's maps and writings which had come into his possession. In 1480, while they were living in Porto Santo, their first son, Diego, was born (Morison 1:51, 59n19).

By 1481, however, Columbus again became restless. He learned that the Portuguese had sailed far enough south to reach the Gold Coast of Africa near the equator. This was essentially the only known part of the Atlantic to which Christopher had not yet sailed. Therefore, during the time he was living in the Madeiras, he made at least one trip to the African Gold Coast. While Columbus was there, he was able to observe for himself that people were actually able to live near the equator. This observation dispelled a myth he had read earlier which maintained that the equatorial zone was uninhabitable because of excessive heat (Phillips and Phillips 106).

With this voyage, Christopher became the most widely travelled seaman of his day. During the years he sailed the Mediterranean, he had been to such diverse places as Chios, Tunis and Marseilles. Now, having moved to Portugal and the Madeiras, he could boast of experience sailing in the Atlantic, to Iceland in the north and to the Gold Coast of Africa in the south. Las Casas claimed: "Columbus was the most outstanding sailor in the world, versed like no other in the art of navigation, for which divine Providence chose him to accomplish the most outstanding feat ever accomplished in the world until now" (Las Casas 17). Now Columbus was ready to plan for an expedition to the Indies, a leap of faith, that would thrust his name, forever, into the annals of history.

Beginnings of a Daring Plan

It was during this period of time that Columbus began to formulate his plan for the great "Enterprise of the Indies," his dream of reaching the East by sailing west. One of the most pertinent questions concerning this plan is: what information was available to Christopher which helped him develop and refine the grand idea? We do know that, while he lived in Portugal, Columbus became an avid student of the Bible and of the writings of prominent theologians, philosophers, mathematicians, geographers and world travelers. He made literally hundreds of notes in the margins of the books that he read, giving insight as to which writings impressed him the most.

Besides the Bible, his other favorite books were Pierre d'Ailly's *Imago Mundi* (Image of the World), Pope Pius II's *Historia Rerum* (History of the World), and Marco Polo's *Description of the World* (Morison 1:120). Of these three works, d'Ailly's *Imago Mundi*, which summarizes geographical thought of the fifteenth-century, evidently had the greatest influence on Columbus' understanding of world geography. His copy of the book is now housed in the Columbus Library in Seville, Spain. In this single volume, Christopher made at least 898 marginal notes, reflecting his great interest in the message of the text (West 2:746).

Many passages in *Imago Mundi* give the impression that the Eurasian continent spans most of the circumference of the earth and that the ocean, therefore, is not particularly broad. Columbus' notes indicate that he was eager to embrace any statement in the work which would advance this theory. He took note of the following statements:

> The end of the habitable earth toward the Orient [east] and the end of the habitable earth toward the Occident [west] are near enough, and between them is a small sea.
>
> Between the end of Spain and the beginning of India is no great width.
>
> An arm of the sea extends between India and Spain.
>
> India is near Spain.
>
> The beginnings of the Orient and of the Occident are close.
>
> From the end of the Occident to the end of India *by land* is much greater than half the globe.

> Aristotle [says] between the end of Spain and the beginning of India is a small sea navigable in a few days...Esdras [says] six parts [of the globe] are habitable and the seventh is covered with water.
>
> The end of Spain and the beginning of India are not far distant but close, and it is evident *that this sea is navigable in a few days with a fair wind.* (Morison 1:122–23, 128n33, n35; emphasis added)

With such a body of statements to support his plan, it is not surprising that Columbus soon became convinced of the feasibility of his strategy for sailing to the Indies.

Christopher's study of Marco Polo's *Description of the World* further supported the conclusions he had drawn from d'Ailly's writings and added fire to his imagination. Polo's book highlights his travels in the Orient in the early fourteenth century, and recounts the marvels of the Grand Khan and of the island of Japan (Cipangu), which Marco Polo said lay 1500 miles off the coast of China. Some scholars doubted the accuracy of this geography, but Columbus was compelled to believe his account that the eastern edge of Asia lay much closer to Europe, by sea, than other men believed (Morison 1:46).

Paolo Toscanelli was one of the few scholars during Columbus' time who approved of Marco Polo. This prestigious Florentine physician was also destined to play an important role in encouraging Christopher to carry out his grand idea. In 1474, the king of Portugal invited Toscanelli to write the crown a letter developing his views on the possibility of travelling to the Indies by sailing westward on the Atlantic Ocean. When Columbus heard of this correspondence, he naturally became interested and wrote to Toscanelli personally. The physician was kind enough to send Christopher a copy of the letter and a sea-chart which he had previously forwarded to the king.

While no one knows where this chart is, a copy of Toscanelli's letter describing it can be found in Ferdinand's biography of his father (Ferdinand 19–22). Toscanelli's map is reported to have shown the west coasts of Europe and Africa, to the extent that they had been explored by the Portuguese up to that time. It also contained a description of the east coast of

Asia, including Japan and the east Asian islands as they existed in Toscanelli's concept of the world. He drew the Atlantic Ocean between Europe and Africa, on the eastern portion of the map, and Asia, on the western portion and superimposed a grid system of parallel lines over the drawing; each grid square supposedly covering a distance of 250 miles. The American continents, of course, were not on the chart, but Toscanelli did include a depiction of the fictitious Antillia island (the Island of the Seven Cities), which was thought to have existed in the middle of the Ocean Sea. The mapmaker believed that one could sail from Lisbon to China "with all security" (Ferdinand 21), and that the voyage could be broken at both the mythical island of Antillia and later, the island of Japan. Columbus agreed that a person could safely sail to the Indies and used Toscanelli's letter and sea-chart as evidence when he attempted to sell his plan to the monarchs of Europe (Morison 1:46).

It is important to note that, even though Columbus used the writings of d'Ailly, Polo, Toscanelli, and others as evidence to support and refine his plan, he never claimed that he derived his grand idea from any of them. Instead he sincerely credited the Lord for the inspiration for the Enterprise of the Indies. He wrote: "I have searched out and studied all kinds of texts: geographies, histories, chronologies, philosophies and other subjects. With a hand that could be felt, *the Lord opened my mind to the fact that it would be possible to sail from here to the Indies*, and he opened my will to desire to accomplish the project" (West and Kling 105; emphasis added).

Armed with a collection of authoritative statements to substantiate his plan, Columbus was now prepared to seek royal sponsorship for his enterprise. Inasmuch as he had lived in Portugal for the last eight years and even married into nobility from that country, Columbus chose, first, to present his plan to the Portuguese crown. In 1484 Christopher gained an audience with John II, who had become king of Portugal in 1481 (Earenfight 1:396).

King John thought enough of Christopher's enterprise to refer it to a maritime commission, headed by Diogo Ortiz. Unfortunately the members of the commission recommended that the plan be rejected, but it was not because they believed the world was flat. Scholars in literally all of the major universities of Europe at that time taught that the earth was round. The flat-earth myth is a fable that refuses to die in an otherwise enlightened world (Russell 1–11). The problem in 1484 was that most learned men believed the sea distance between Europe and the Indies was so great that it would be impossible to make the voyage without first running out of provisions. Furthermore, even if the voyage could be made, they felt it would be financially impractical to attempt it. The commission consequently rejected the proposal, believing that the idea was "vain, simply founded on imagination, or on things like that Isle Cypango of Marco Polo" (Morison 1:94).

This rejection, coupled with the fact that his wife, Felipa, had recently died, was most disheartening to Columbus. He, therefore, decided that he and his five-year-old son, Diego, would move to Spain in search of a better life. It was in Spain that this visionary man from Genoa would finally obtain the royal support he needed to fulfill his divine mission.

CHAPTER FOUR

Years In Spain: Columbus Finds a Sponsor

The Lord purposed that there should be something clearly miraculous in this matter of the voyage to the Indies . . . I spent seven years here in your royal court discussing this subject with the leading persons in all learned arts, and their conclusion was that it was vain. . . . But afterwards it all turned out just as our redeemer Jesus Christ has said, and as he had spoken earlier by the mouth of his holy prophets.

—Christopher Columbus

In 1485 Christopher Columbus, in company with his young son, Diego, took passage on a ship from Lisbon to Palos, Spain. As their ship neared its destination, it passed by a beautiful monastery located on a bluff overlooking the sea. This monastery, named La Rábida, soon became an extremely important sanctuary for Columbus. It served as a home for Diego while Christopher was away promoting his plan (Ferdinand 37). It was here that Columbus was also befriended by influential and learned churchmen, such as Antonio de Marchena and Juan Pérez, who were sympathetic and helpful to him in his inspired cause (Morison 1:108; see also Taviana, *The Grand Design*, 168–70; 433–38). And equally important, La Rábida became a spiritual refuge for Christopher himself.

A Desire to Spread Christianity

With this religious setting as a backdrop, it now seems appropriate to consider one of the most important, yet least discussed, themes in Columbus' life: his spiritual motive for sailing to the Indies. It has become the vogue in this materialistic age to say that Christopher's primary motivation was economic. For example, a recent article in a popular American magazine maintains that "the Enterprise of the Indies . . . was a business trip. His chief motive was one of the oldest and most powerful of all: money" (Carlinsky 52). Columbus was a complex individual and, no doubt, had multiple motives for what he did. After all, people rarely have only one motive for the things that they do in life. However, simply to say that Christopher's chief motivation was economic distorts the truth and hides from the reader an important role that he said he played, that of being the "Christ-bearer."

Sources on Christopher's life are replete with evidence that one of his major motivations to sail to the Indies was to spread Christianity. He once wrote the following to Amerigo Vespucci (the explorer for whom America is named): "I feel persuaded by the many and wonderful manifestations of Divine Providence in my especial favour, that I am the chosen instrument of God in bringing to pass a great event—no less than the conversion of millions who are now existing in the darkness of Paganism" (Lester 79).

Many of the books that Columbus read and annotated addressed this theme. In the prologue in his personal copy of Marco Polo's *Description of the World*, its translator, Francesco Pipino, argued the book's usefulness for converting "pagans" (Jones 2:557).

Columbus' copy of *Imago Mundi* by Pierre d'Ailly contains a number of ideas which greatly influenced Christopher's thinking. He read there that the earth, as we know it, would have a lifespan of 7,000 years: "Saint Augustine says that the end of the world will take place in the seventh millennium after the age of the creation of the world. The theologians of the Church follow this view, in particular, Cardinal Petrus Aliacus [Pierre d'Ailly]" (West and Kling 109). After reading the Cardinal's estimate of the number of years from the creation of the world until Jesus' mortal ministry, Columbus added the years from the time of Christ to his own time. He then concluded that a little more than a century and a half remained before the end of the world. This deduction gave him a sense of great urgency because he had read in the Bible that Christianity would need to be taken to all nations, kindreds, and tongues before the end of the world. The fact that Christopher was obsessed with the final conversion of all the world before the Second Coming of the Savior is reflected in his repeated attention to John 10:16, which he was fond of quoting: "And other sheep I have that are not of this fold: them also I must bring, and they shall hear my voice: and there shall be one fold and one shepherd" (Watts 93; West and Kling 229).

In his two letters to Columbus, Paolo Toscanelli spoke of the importance of spreading Christianity. In the first letter, he said that the predecessors of the Great Khan of Cathay (China), "greatly desired to have friendship and dealings with the Christians, and about two hundred years ago they sent ambassadors to the Pope, asking for many learned men and teachers to instruct them in our faith; but these ambassadors, encountering obstacles on the way, turned back without reaching Rome" (Ferdinand 21). Toscanelli claimed, however, that "in the time of Pope Eugenius there came to him an ambassador [from China] who told of their great feeling of friendship for the Christians" (Ibid). In his second letter, Toscanelli maintained that the Enterprise would "be a voyage to kings and princes who are very eager to have friendly dealings and speech with the Christians of our countries. . . . They are also very eager to know and speak with the learned men of our lands concerning religion" (Ibid 22).

Contemporary accounts of Columbus spoke matter-of-factly of his going to the Indies to carry the message of Christ to the inhabitants of the lands he encountered. Las Casas proclaimed that, "the discovery of the New World was one of the most outstanding exploits reserved by God for the propagation of his holy Church over so extensive a part of the universe hitherto hidden, and for the resplendence of His holy Faith among an infinite number of nations" (Las Casas 30).

It seems clear that the Spanish monarchs also shared at least a part of Columbus' enthusiasm for spreading the message of Christ. The first entry in Christopher's journal of the maiden voyage stated, "Because of the report that I had given to Your Highnesses [Ferdinand and Isabella] about the lands of India and about a prince who is called 'Grand Khan' . . . Your Highnesses . . . lovers and promoters of the Holy Christian faith . . . thought of sending me, Christóbal Colón, to the said regions of India to see the said princes and the peoples and lands . . . *to see how their conversion to our Holy Faith might be undertaken*" (Dunn and Kelly 17, 19; emphasis added).

While Columbus did not have access to the fulness of the Restored Gospel, his efforts, nevertheless, would result in the reintroduction of Christianity to the descendants of Lehi then living in the Americas. This missionary effort, as we know, helped prepare the way for eventual acceptance of the fulness of the gospel after it was restored in the latter days. In this way, Columbus' proselyting ambitions helped to accomplish the Lord's purposes.

Elder B.H. Roberts wrote of the role played by people of other faiths in the accomplishment of the Lord's designs, making it clear that he believed contributors from outside the Church assist in divine purposes: "God raises up wise men and prophets here and there among all the children of men . . . speaking to them through means that they can comprehend; not always giving a fulness of truth such as may be found in the fulness of the gospel of Jesus Christ; but always giving that measure of truth that the people are prepared to receive." He also noted that "Wherever God finds a soul sufficiently enlightened and pure; one with whom his Spirit can communicate, lo! he makes of him a teacher of men." (Roberts 512–13; emphasis added). An official statement of the First Presidency in 1978 further validates this view. Issued during the administration of President Spencer W. Kimball, this declaration clearly states that great men and women in the history of the world have "received a portion of God's light. Moral truths were given to them by God to enlighten whole nations and to bring a higher level of understanding to individuals" (Palmer 208). Given his desires to spread the message of Christ and his part as the initiator of Christian missionary work in the New World, Columbus surely fits into this classification of inspired individuals who have helped lay the foundation for the fulness of the Restored Gospel.

In Seach of a Sponsor

Feeling enthusiastic about spreading Christianity and optimistic about obtaining sponsorship in Spain, Columbus presented his plan to the Spanish crown in 1486. At that time, King Ferdinand of Aragon and Queen Isabella of Castile were ruling over much of the land that has since become Spain. Their marriage, in 1469, was an initial step in the eventual creation of a unified Spain. They were usually referred to as the Spanish monarchs or the Catholic sovereigns. These two monarchs would eventually play a vitally important role in the Enterprise of the Indies, and their names would go down in history, forever associated with that of Christopher Columbus.

Isabella was a beautiful woman with a healthy, clear complexion, auburn hair and blue eyes. She was a truly religious person with uncommonly high morals. The queen's gracious, dignified and tactful manner endeared her to her subjects and helped make her an exceptionally capable ruler. She did, in fact, rule Castile while Ferdinand ruled Aragón (Phillips and Phillips 112–13). Isabella and Columbus were the same age and seemed to like each other, and his desire to spread Christianity appealed to her pious nature (Morison 1:114–15).

Ferdinand, on the other hand, was not as genial as Isabella, but was a strong, energetic, ambitious ruler who prided himself on being a shrewd diplomat; he played a role in virtually every political alliance on the European continent (Morison 1:114). Columbus would attract Ferndinand's attention by projecting the political and financial rewards to be captured by the Enterprise.

In May of 1486, Columbus approached the Crown with his grand idea. The monarchs received his presentation open-mindedly and referred his recommendations to a maritime commission headed by Fray Hernando de Talavera, the queen's confessor. Columbus appeared before the commission, but a division among the involved scholars prevented a quick answer on the matter. After months of dawdling deliberation, the commission eventually issued its first unfavorable decision. As a result, the Crown ruled that the Enterprise should be postponed indefinitely, but Columbus was retained in 1487 as an agent of the court at a salary of approximately 1000 maravedis per month (Morison 1:117–18). An important consideration in the decision was, no doubt, the fact that Spain was deeply involved in a war to remove the Moors from Granada in the south of present-day Spain; King Ferdinand and Queen Isabella were generally preoccupied with this campaign and were uncertain of the country's ability to finance other ventures at this same time. Thus began a six-year waiting period for Columbus, a time which was, perhaps, the most difficult of his life because of the uncertainty of the fate of his plan and his career.

The year 1488 was one of turmoil and frustration for Christopher. By June, the Spanish monarchs had apparently lost interest in him and his plan; they terminated his retaining fee, an action that possibly persuaded him to accept King John's invitation to return to Portugal. In the middle of this latest setback, Columbus' second son, Ferdinand, was born in August 1488 to Beatriz Enriquez de Harana (also spelled Arana), to whom Columbus was never married. Although there is much conjecture on the matter, no one knows why they never married.

The records do show that Columbus did have their son declared "legitimate" and provided for Beatriz in his will (see Morison 1:111–13; Taviani, *Grand Design*, 468–72; and West and West 35).

By December of 1488, we see Columbus back in Lisbon promoting his plan among the Portuguese. As it turned out, he returned to Lisbon at a most inopportune time. Bartholomew Dias had just returned from his successful circumnavigation of the Cape of Good Hope at the southern tip of Africa, a maritime breakthrough of major proportion: that provided King John with an ocean route to India. Consequently, the Portuguese court lost enthusiasm for Columbus' theoretical western route (Morison 1:118).

Almost simultaneously, Christopher dispatched his brother Bartholomew to the court of Henry VII of England, in hopes of persuading the British to sponsor the Enterprise. Finding Henry to be either apathetic toward the plan, or stubborn in bargaining over the price of the expedition, Bartholomew evidently left England and proceeded to the court of King Charles VIII of France. Apparently, Charles also had little interest in the Enterprise, but his sister, Anne de Beaujeu, the king's regent during his minority, reacted favorably to Bartholomew's propositions and encouraged him to stay in France, retaining him as a mapmaker (Morison 1:118–19).

While Bartholomew courted the monarchs of England and France, Columbus returned to Spain from Lisbon and, in 1490, made another appeal to Ferdinand and Isabella. According to Las Casas, they referred the proposal to Talavera and his committee again who, after a cursory review, declared that the idea was "impossible and vain and worthy of rejection" (Morison 1:131). The monarchs, however, did not act on Talavera's report, but rather advised Christopher that he should again submit his proposal at a more timely juncture—namely, at the conclusion of the war in Granada.

Columbus waited several more months for the opportunity to re-submit his plan, but then lost patience with Ferdinand and

Isabella. Dejected he decided to go to France to join his brother in soliciting Charles' support for the Enterprise. However, while Columbus was at the monastery of La Rábida, where he had gone to visit his son Diego, Fray Juan Pérez persuaded him not to abandon Spain, but to make one more attempt. Pérez, who had previously served as the queen's confessor, then arranged for another audience with the Spanish monarchs in 1491. Isabella sent a letter requesting Columbus' presence at court, also forwarding a sum of 20,000 maravedis for him to procure some presentable clothes and a mule for transportation (Morison 1:133).

Dressed in a new suit, Columbus arrived at the Royal Court, this time at Santa Fe, in August 1491 or soon thereafter. He again made the now-familiar presentation of the Enterprise of the Indies, including his demands for formal hereditary titles and financial remuneration, all to be conferred on the successful completion of the expedition. Among other things, he asked for the following: first, the hereditary titles of Viceroy and Governor over all lands to be discovered on the voyage; second, the office of Admiral of the Ocean Sea, also to be passed on to his descendants forever; and, third, one-tenth of all the gold, silver, pearls, gems, spices and other merchandise produced in the lands to be discovered (Curtis 1:182; see also Morison 1:139). Once again, the monarchs referred the plan to a committee.

Columbus had every reason to believe that the king and queen would finally accept his grand idea on this attempt. On 2 January 1492, while he was waiting for an answer, Spain defeated the Moors in Granada. This, at last, made it possible for Ferdinand and Isabella to give their attention to other matters. They probably would have accepted Christopher's proposal this time but they thought his price was too high, his demands for hereditary titles and revenues being too extravagant (Ferdinand 42). Consequently, Ferdinand and Isabella rejected the plan once again. This was the last straw for Columbus; he decided to leave Spain forever and join his brother in France.

He packed his new mule and rode for Cordova, planning to work his way to France if he hadn't saved enough of the queen's present to pay for passage. However, providence intervened, stopping his flight and changing his fortune forever. As Columbus fled the court in Santa Fe, Luis de Santangel, financial advisor to the crown, persuaded Queen Isabella to change her mind at the last moment. He reasoned that the Enterprise, "offered so little risk yet *could prove of so great service to God and the exaltation of His Church*, not to speak of the very great increase and glory of her realms and kingdoms" (Ferdinand 43; emphasis added). The queen was so impressed with Santangel's enthusiasm and sincerity that she even offered to pledge her jewels in order to finance the Enterprise. The finance minister assured her that so great a sacrifice would not be necessary, and the monarchs finally approved the plan (Ferdinand 44). In the end, the crown granted Columbus everything he had asked for all to be conferred, of course, upon the successful completion of the Enterprise. Columbus' achievement was made all the more incredible by the fact that he was not even of Spanish birth.

After eight years of frustration, dating back to his first attempt to gain financial backing in Portugal, Christopher Columbus had a royal sponsor for his grand idea. Providence had finally blessed his dogged determination. He attributed the monarchs' capitulation to divine intercession, exclaiming, "I spent seven years here in your royal court discussing this subject with the leading persons in all the learned arts, and their conclusion was that all was in vain. That was the end, and they gave it up. But afterwards it all turned out just as our redeemer Jesus Christ had said, and as he had spoken earlier by the mouth of his holy prophets" (West and Kling 107). Christopher was now ready to embark upon the most celebrated sea voyage theretofore attempted in the history of the world, his Enterprise of the Indies.

CHAPTER FIVE

First Voyage to the Americas: Columbus Guided by the Spirit

With a hand that could be felt, the Lord opened my mind to the fact that it would be possible to sail from here to the Indies. . . . This was a fire that burned within me. . . . who can doubt that this fire was not merely mine, but also of the Holy Spirit.

—Christopher Columbus

The anticipation and drama associated with Christopher Columbus' first expedition to the Americas is almost unparalleled in human history. Perhaps the only event of comparable magnitude in our day was man's first landing on the moon in 1969. Inasmuch as Columbus sailed 33 continuous days into the unknown, with a crew on the verge of mutiny in the final stages, it is apparent that every decision he made was crucial to both the success of his expedition and the survival of his small fleet. It is amazing, said George E. Nunn, a prominent geographer, that Christopher "did not make a single false move in the entire voyage" (Nunn 43). To what can we attribute such incredible seafaring precision, and what were the Admiral's inner-most thoughts and feelings during the voyage? The answers to these questions lie in the several accounts of the journey that have endured the five centuries since that stunning expedition.

Map of First Voyage

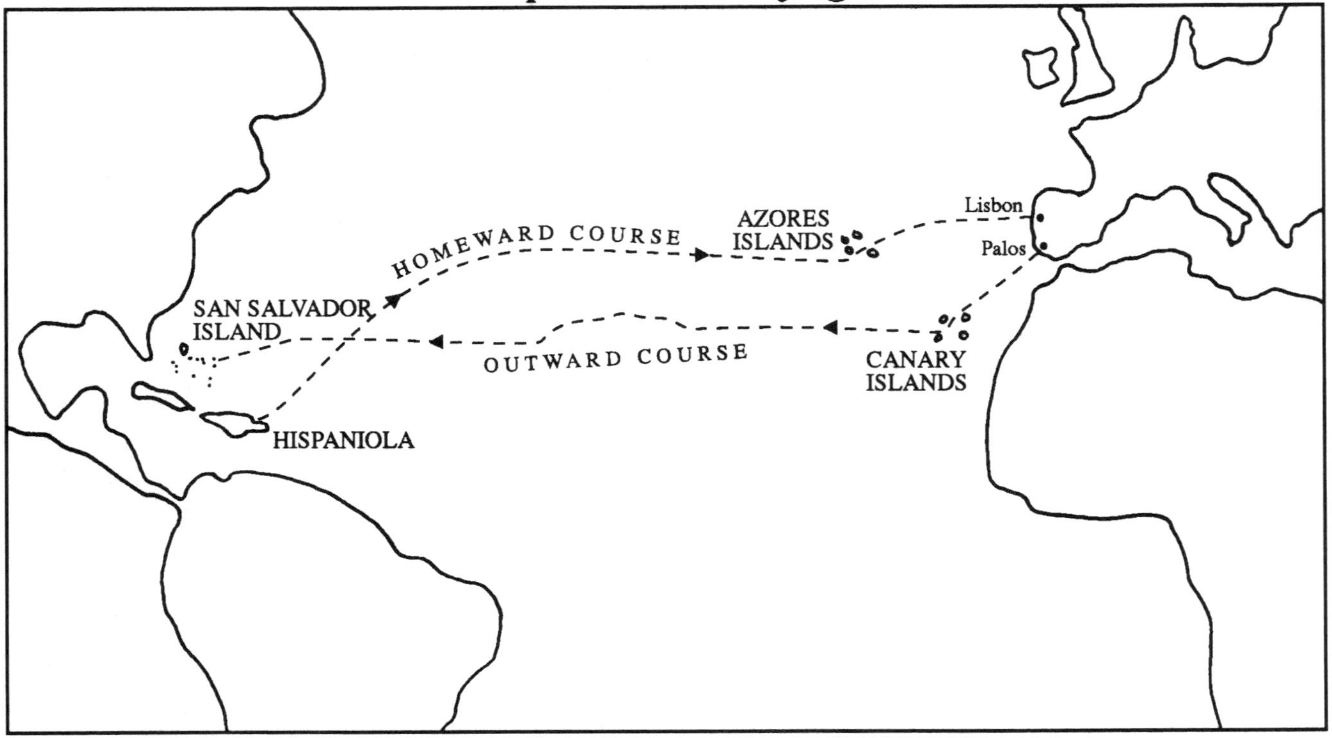

Historians have written about Columbus' first voyage to America from many points of view. Most secular historians, however, have placed little emphasis on the most important theme of all—the fact that Columbus was guided by the Spirit of God. Beginning with the decision Christopher made concerning his point of departure, and continuing all the way through to his return voyage to Spain, we can find numerous junctures at which the Lord manifested His hand in Columbus' key decisions.

Before 1492, other navigators had tried unsuccessfully to explore westward from the Azores Islands (800 miles west of the coast of Portugal), assuming that this was the best place from which to set sail (Morison 1:97–98). Although the Azores were the western-most islands known in the Atlantic, Columbus chose to sail from Palos, Spain, to the Canary Islands (off the west coast of Africa) and from there, to launch his voyage into the vast unknown. By doing so, he caught the tradewinds blowing from the northeast to the southwest and avoided the headwinds which blow from the west to the east in the vicinity of the Azores (Nunn 37–38, 42).

The route Columbus chose has stood the test of time: five hundred years of sailing have proven it the best possible course for sailing west from southern Europe to North America. Nunn suggested that Columbus' successful navigation was the result of "an application of reason to . . . knowledge" (Nunn 50). Columbus, however, gave credit to the Lord. Even though he was a successful seaman and an accomplished navigator, he said, "With a hand that could be felt, the Lord opened my mind to the fact that it would be possible to sail from here to the Indies" (West and Kling 105).

Inspirational Junctures

Columbus experienced relatively easy sailing during the entire outward voyage; had he not done so, he likely would not have reached America before his crew mutinied. There was one occasion, however, on 23 September, when the sea became

Course Changes of the First Voyage

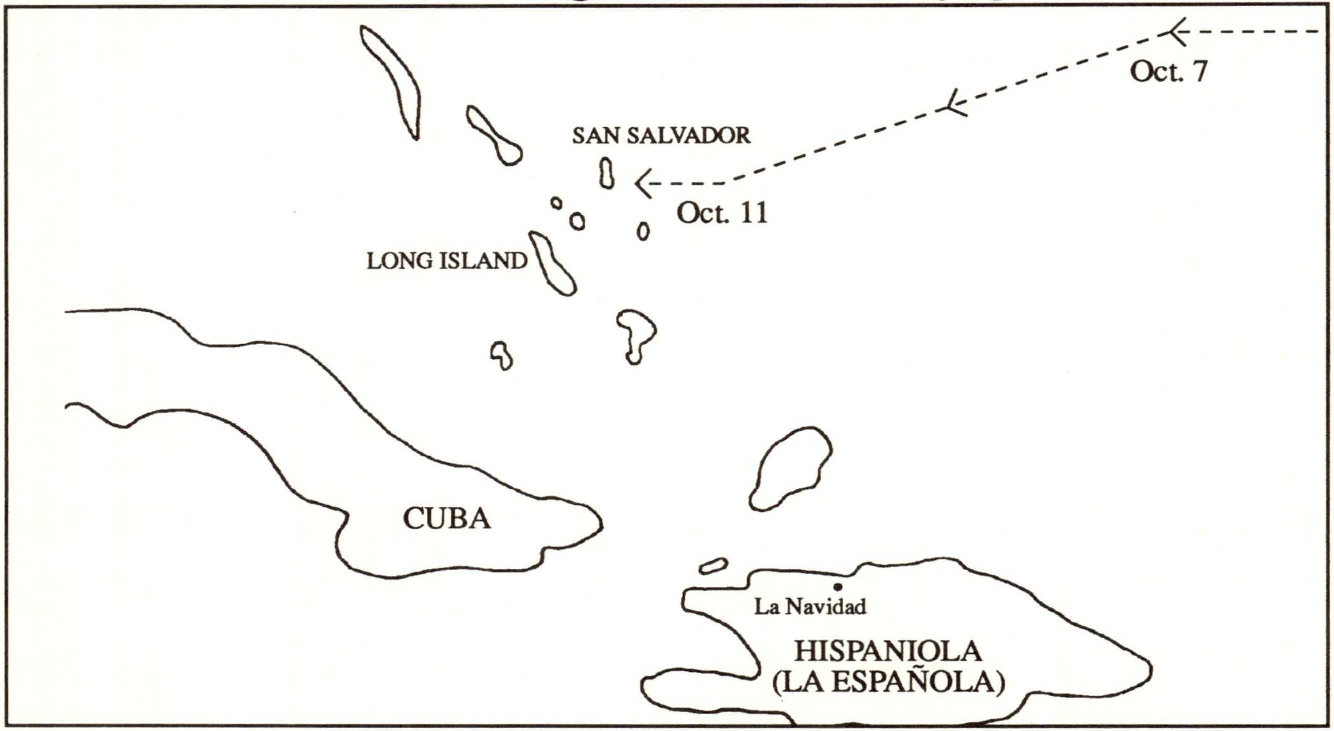

calm, and the ships were stalled for part of the day. Columbus noted in his journal that the crew, which had not seen land for some days, began to complain that since there were no heavy seas in the region, the wind would never blow hard enough to return to Spain. Soon thereafter, the sea mysteriously rose without wind, astonishing the crew (Dunn and Kelly 41). The Admiral considered this a divine miracle. He said, "the high sea was very necessary to me, [a sign] which had not appeared except in the time of the Jews when they left Egypt [and complained] against Moses, who took them out of captivity" (Ibid).

On the way to America, Columbus changed course only twice during the entire 33 days at sea. The first alteration was on 7 October. Until that time, Christopher had sailed due west for 28 days. Then he noted in his journal that a great multitude of birds passed over, going from north to southwest. Bartolomé de Las Casas, the man who transcribed Columbus' journal, wrote that from this observation, the Admiral "decided to alter course and turn the prow to the WSW [west southwest]" (Fuson 71). Professor Morison claimed that if Columbus had not changed course, "the voyage would have taken a day longer" (Morison 1:283). That extra day would have been critical, since two days before the eventual sighting of land, the crew threatened mutiny. Every extra day at sea heightened their anxiety; the Admiral's time-saving change of course on 7 October, therefore, just may have saved the expedition.

The story of the threatened mutiny is one of the most dramatic episodes of the first voyage. The incident took place on Wednesday, 10 October 1492, after they had been at sea for over 31 days without seeing land. The sailors, who had been concealing their discontent, now openly threatened insurrection. They had come to believe that Columbus, the foreigner from Genoa, had deceived them; they supposed he was leading them on a journey from which they would never return. According to one account, the sailors even conspired to do away with their leader, whom they "planned to throw into the sea" (d'-

Anghera 1:59–60). Yet, "Columbus, by using gentle words, holding out promises and flattering their hopes, sought to gain time, and he succeeded in calming their fears" (Ibid). Others have stated, after the fact, that at this juncture, Columbus promised the men that they would return if they did not sight land within two or three days (Morison 1:286, 290–91, 292n6). Although Columbus did not record this oft-repeated assertion in his journal, he did report that "I also told the men that it was useless to complain, for I had started out to find the Indies and would continue until I had accomplished that mission, *with the help of Our Lord*" (Fuson 72; emphasis added). This incident serves as an excellent example of Columbus' determination and faith in God.

The second instance in which the Admiral altered his route was after sunset on 11 October, just a few hours before land was sighted. For no apparent reason, he gave orders to change direction from west southwest back to the original course of due west (Dunn and Kelly 59). He gave no explanation for the change, but it was, nevertheless, an excellent choice. Had he continued on the west southwest course instead of steering due west, he would have missed the island of San Salvador, and would likely have ended up on the deadly reefs along the coast of Long Island (in the Caribbean), perhaps never returning to Spain (Morison 1:295). Many historians have attributed these changes in course to luck or chance, but Las Casas said, "God gave this man the keys to the awesome seas, he and no other unlocked the darkness" (Las Casas 35), and I agree.

Having made this second course correction, Columbus was then right on target, and just in time to meet with his destiny—to discover the New Land. That evening as the crew gathered for prayer, the Admiral, "spoke to the men of the favor that [the] Lord had shown them by conducting them so safely and prosperously with fair winds and a clear course, and by comforting them with signs that daily grew more abundant" (Ferdinand 58). His policy since reaching a point 700 leagues beyond the Canaries had been not to sail at night, but the crew's desire to see land was so great that Columbus decided to sail through the darkness (Morison 1:294). He commanded the night watch to keep an especially sharp lookout because he was confident that land was nearby. In addition to an annuity of 10,000 maravedis guaranteed by the Sovereigns, the Admiral also promised to give a silk jacket to the first sailor who sighted land (Dunn and Kelly 63).

About 10 o'clock that night, Columbus saw a light in the distant dark, but it was so faint that he did not publicly announce it. He did, however, bring it to the attention of Pedro Gutiérrez, who also acknowledged seeing the flickering light. Rodrigo Sánchez was also called on to observe the light, but he claimed he could see nothing from where he was (Phillips and Phillips 153). Notwithstanding Columbus' glimpse of the light, it was some four hours later, at about two in the morning on 12 October, that the fleet sighted land for certain. Rodrigo de Triana, a sailor on the *Pinta*, shouted, "*Tierra! tierra*!", while the fleet was still two leagues off shore (Morison 1:298). Martín Pinzón, the captain of the *Pinta*, quickly verified Triana's claim and then fired a cannon shot, which was the prearranged signal for sighting land.

One can only imagine the gratitude and relief they all must have felt, after more than a month of anxious days at sea, when their eyes first saw this obscure little island in the middle of the tropical Caribbean Sea. It goes without saying that the crews were ecstatic and their respect and admiration for the Admiral soared, literally, overnight.

For Columbus, this historic sighting was a rendezvous with destiny. He had proven, in spite of mounting opposition and a lack of faith on the part of his crew, that it was possible to sail westward across the great Atlantic . According to his agreement with the monarchs, Columbus officially became Admiral of the Ocean Sea, simultaneously gaining the titles of Viceroy and Governor of this island at the moment he discovered it. Professor Hugh Nibley aptly put this celebrated moment into proper perspective when he said: "Everything else in Columbus' life is subservient to the carrying out of that one mission. The aim and purpose of all his work and suffering was what happened at 2 a.m. on the morning of October 12, 1492" (Nibley 320).

Impatient and anxious to explore their new discovery, the crew waited through the night, and sailed excitedly to shore at daybreak. Upon reaching dry ground, the landing party knelt, kissed the sand with tears of joy, and offered prayers of thanks to God. Rising from his knees, the Admiral named the island San Salvador (Holy Savior), thus beginning a personal tradition of giving names of religious significance to many newly discovered lands (Ferdinand 59). In deference to the crown, Columbus dedicated San Salvador, which lay off the northern coast of Cuba, to the Spanish monarchs.

Exploring the Wonders of the Caribbean

The arrival of the ships did not go unnoticed by the inhabitants of the island. Many of the natives soon gathered at the crew's landing site. Columbus observed that, "All of them go around as naked as their mothers bore them; and the women also, although I did not see more than one quite young girl. And all those that I saw were young people, for none did I see of more than 30 years of age. They are very well formed, with handsome bodies and good faces. Their hair [is] coarse—almost like the tail of a horse—and short" (Dunn and Kelly 65–66).

The Admiral's faithful motive for making the voyage is quickly revealed by his impressions on meeting the island people. He confided, "I recognized that they were people who would be better freed [from error] and converted to our Holy Faith by love than by force" (Ibid 65). Later in his journal, Columbus noted: "I believe that they would become Christians very easily, for it seemed to me that they had no religion" (Ibid 69). He determined to take six of the islanders with him in order to educate them in Spanish and in the ways of European life.

After three days of exploring on San Salvador, the Admiral set sail southward, passing various islands en route to an eventual landing at Cuba on 28 October. An astonishing reception awaited the Spanish explorers at this port. Columbus sent two men inland to survey the island's interior, and they returned with an inspirational account. Arriving at a village of about 1000 inhabitants 12 leagues from the shore, the men had been greeted with great reverence and adoration: "the Indians touched them and kissed their hands and feet, marveling and believing that the Spaniards came from the heavens" (Dunn and Kelly 137).

Through an Indian interpreter, the village was informed "of the way the Christians lived and that they were good people." Later, the women of the village came toward the two explorers, "kissing their hands and feet and feeling them, attempting to see if they were, like themselves, of flesh and bone" (Ibid). When it came time for the two Spaniards to leave, hundreds of the natives wanted to go with them. Columbus wrote that, "more than 500 men and women would have come with them, because they thought that the Spaniards would return to the heavens" (Ibid).

This account of native Americans giving reverence to the fair-skinned men whom they believed had come from heaven is intriguing to those who believe in the Book of Mormon. The Indians' adoration for these men undoubtedly came from their belief in the legend of the bearded white God. Of course many Latter-day Saints believe that this legend is based on the Book of Mormon account in 3 Nephi of Christ's appearance in ancient America after his resurrection.

Paul Cheesman in *The World of the Book of Mormon* claimed: "The bearded white God is one of the most universally taught and accepted legends of the Indians of North and South America. Virtually all tribes teach of him. Tribal songs, dances, and sacred rituals are dedicated to his name" (Cheesman 7). Even though the white God's "name varies from tribe to tribe, his description and teachings are basically the same. In each tribe, in song and story, he was described as white and fair, with long brown hair and a beard"(Ibid). Cheesman further stated that the God's "message was of love and peace. He announced to the people that he was born of a virgin. And, last of all, He promised to return" (Ibid). Because this legend was part of their culture, it is little wonder that the native Americans of Cuba sincerely believed that Columbus' fair-skinned sailors literally came from heaven and were, therefore, worthy of reverence and adoration.

Christopher was so impressed with the spiritual potential of the Indians that he made an immediate plea on their behalf in his journal that day: "I truly believe, most Serene Princes . . . that, given devout religious persons knowing thoroughly the language that they use, soon all of them would become Christian." Continuing his petition to the monarchs, he pleaded, "I hope in Our Lord that Your Highnesses, with much diligence, will decide to send such persons in order to bring to the Church such great nations and to convert them" (Dunn and Kelley 141). These requests, made at a time of such personal accomplishment, further illuminate Christopher's great devotion to things spiritual; the informed reader can not doubt that he was truly motivated by his desire to serve God.

Unfortunately, not all of the crew's discoveries on Cuba were of a spiritual nature: it was there that the Admiral's men first saw the Indians smoke tobacco, an experience that eventually led to its introduction to Europe and the rest of the world. Written forty years after the fact, Las Casas' account of the sailors' experience with tobacco is humorous: he wrote that the Spaniards were then beginning to take up smoking, "although I know not what taste or profit they find in it" (Morison 1:342).

Columbus spent the entire month of November exploring the northeast coast of Cuba; then, on 5 December 1492, he sailed across the windward passage and safely made his way to the island of Hispaniola. The climate and trees of this new land reminded him so much of Spain that he decided to name it Española (Dunn and Kelly 215). However, as early as 1494, Peter Martyr, the first New World historian, began referring to the island as Hispaniola, its Latin name, by which it is still known today (Morison 1:370, 383n5). Haiti and the Dominican Republic are the two countries currently on the island. This island would soon become the home of the first Spanish colony in the New World. Unfortunately, it would also be the scene of much frustration, tribulation, and humiliation for Columbus.

The Admiral's first Christmas in America was not destined to be a merry one. Instead, it was the date of a major calamity on this historic voyage. On the days just prior to Christmas, while the fleet was exploring the shores of Hispaniola, the weather had been turbulent making it difficult for the crew to sleep. Then on Christmas Eve the weather finally turned calm. After some Christmas festivities, the tired crew settled in for a restful night's sleep. Unfortunately, the helmsman was also sleepy and turned the tiller over to a boy, even though Columbus had specifically ordered the crew not to allow a boy to steer the ship (Dunn and Kelley 277).

Disaster struck just before midnight on Christmas Eve as the *Santa María* slid upon a coral reef so gently that the crew was not even aware that they were aground. Nevertheless, the boy knew what had happened as soon as he felt the rudder lodge in the coral (Taviani, *The Great Adventure*, 130–31). Even though it was not a tumultuous wreck and no lives were lost, the resulting leakage was so severe that the ship was unsalvageable. The accident forced Columbus to abandon the wreckage, and he was obliged to leave 39 of his crew in a make-shift fort built from what was left of the ship. This fort, named *La Navidad* because of their arrival on Christmas day, became the first Spanish colony in the New World, although it came about quite by chance. The crew members that were left behind to await the Admiral's return on his next voyage were more than willing to stay, because they would have the first chance at discovering gold, a dream which served to motivate many of the sailors (Morison 1: 393–94).

The Homeward Voyage

After exploring the islands of the Caribbean for three months, Columbus prepared to return to Europe in his substitute flagship, the *Niña*. The route the Admiral chose for his homeward journey is yet another example of his being inspired of God. On 14 January 1493, he recorded in his log, "I have faith in Our Lord that He who brought me here will lead me back in His pity and mercy . . . no one else was supportive of me except God, because He knew my heart" (Fuson 174). Columbus did not return to Spain by the same southern sea passage that had carried him to America. Instead, he sailed northeast and caught winds coming out of the west that took him back across the Atlantic to the Azores. Once again, Nunn asserted that Columbus' navigational decisions were remarkable: "So much has been said about his discovery of America that it has been lost to sight and thought that he also discovered both of the great sailing routes in the North Atlantic" (Nunn 50). With no prior trans-Atlantic sailing experience, how did Christopher enjoy such good fortune on both legs of the trip? One noted historian declared, "there can be no doubt that the faith of Columbus was genuine and sincere, and that his frequent communion with forces unseen was a vital element in his achievement" (Morison 1:65).

On 16 January the Admiral began his homeward trek. The unknown winds served him well at first; he experienced relatively smooth sailing for the first four weeks. Then, all of a sudden, it seemed as if the devil himself was attempting to prevent Columbus from achieving his providential destiny. On 12 February, the fleet was overtaken by a violent tempest, perhaps more perilous than any of the other storms the sailors had experienced in their lives. On 14 February, the winds became even more treacherous and Columbus' ship, the *Niña*, became separated from the *Pinta* until their journey's end. The Admiral said, "The winds increased and the waves were frightful, one contrary to the other, so they crossed and held back the vessel which could neither go forward nor get out from between them, and the waves broke on her" (Dunn and Kelly 363–65). The storm was so terrible that none of the men thought they would live through it.

In the midst of this nightmare at sea, Columbus assembled the crew and called on the Lord for help. He ordered all the men on the ship to draw lots to choose one of the crew to take a pilgrimage to Santa María de Guadalupe if the Lord would save their lives and allow them to return to Spain. For the drawing, Christopher put a chick-pea into a hat for each member of the crew, with one pea marked with a cross. Columbus drew first and, as fate would have it, he picked the pea with the cross on it. When the storm raged on, Christopher ordered another drawing, this time for a pilgrimage to Santa María de Loreto in Italy. The lot fell on a sailor named Pedro de Villa, and Columbus promised to give him money for his journey. The storm intensified so the Admiral ordered a third drawing, this time for a pilgrimage to Santa Clara de Moguer. Surprisingly, the lot fell once again to him, but the storm did not subside. Finally, they all made a solemn covenant that if the Lord would lead them safely to shore, they would immediately "go in their shirt-sleeves in a procession to pray in a church" (Dunn and Kelly 365–67). That evening the storm began to subside and the next morning they spotted land—they had reached the Azores, 800 miles off the coast of Portugal.

However, the raging sea had not yet finished with the battered ships. After a week's stay in the Azores, the *Niña* set sail for the mainland of Portugal. On 3 March another devastating storm struck, so powerfully that it tore all the ship's sails. Once again the crew drew lots, this time to send a pilgrim in his shirt-sleeves to Santa María de la Cinta in Huelva. Amazingly the lot fell to Columbus again. In addition, all of the men "made a vow to fast on bread and water the first Saturday when they reached land" (Dunn and Kelley 391). The next morning the storm blew them into the mouth of the Lisbon River, and they made their way to a dock. Finally, they arrived at Palos, Spain, on 15 March 1493; and the *Pinta* sailed into the same port just a few hours later. The next month Christopher Columbus appeared before King Ferdinand and Queen Isabella of Spain to give his report. "All the Court and the city came out to meet him; and the Catholic Sovereigns received him in public, seated with all majesty and grandeur on rich thrones under a canopy of cloth of gold. When he came forward to kiss their hands, they rose from their thrones as if he were a great lord, and would not let him kiss their hands but made him sit down beside them" (Ferdinand 101). This reception was a striking contrast from the scene played out the year before, when Columbus left the court in despair after these same monarchs had rejected his proposal.

Thus, with the help of the Lord, Christopher Columbus was able to accomplish one of the greatest feats in human history. After this marvelous achievement, he could have taken all the glory for himself, but throughout his life he consistently gave credit to God. For example, in 1500, he solemnly declared: "Our Lord made me the messenger of the new heaven and the new earth . . . and he showed me the place where to find it" (Brigham, *Life*, 50, 57n5).

The Admiral's encounter with America literally opened the floodgate to explorers, colonizers, fortune seekers, and missionaries. Many of these people would accomplish honorable purposes, while others would, unfortunately, be detrimental. Whatever the final outcome, the world would most certainly never be the same.

CHAPTER SIX

Later Voyages: Columbus as Governor

The world owes most to the men, great and small, who in the name of truth have dared to challenge tradition. . . . Yet, when [Columbus] challenged the geographical tradition of his day, he was scorned by compatriots; and even when he had discovered America, jealousy and misunderstanding landed him in prison and left him brokenhearted. Nevertheless, the great era of geographical exploration and discovery may well be dated from Columbus.

—John A. Widtsoe

Christopher Columbus was certainly at a high point in his life when he returned from his first voyage to the Americas and was honored by King Ferdinand and Queen Isabella. He remained with the royal court at Barcelona for several weeks thereafter. During this time he advised the crown on diplomatic matters, made plans for a second trans-atlantic voyage, interviewed people who wished to sail to the New World, and attended royal social functions (Morison 2:14).

One of the most significant and memorable events that the Admiral attended at this time was the baptism of the six native Americans he had brought back with him from the Indies. Ferdinand, Isabella, and their son, the Infante Don Juan, acted as god-parents to the new converts. They named one Indian after the king, another after Don Juan, and a third, the Admiral's interpreter, they christened Don Diego Colón. "Don Juan" became a part of the royal household, where he was "well behaved and circumspect" according to Oviedo (Morison 2:14). Unfortunately, Don Juan died just two years later. The other five natives returned to the Americas with Columbus on his second voyage.

Another notable function that the Admiral attended during the interlude between the first and second voyages was a magnificent banquet given by Don Pedro Gonzales de Mendoza, Archbishop of Toledo and Grand Cardinal of Spain. Mendoza was a powerful and loyal supporter of the crown, and was probably the most important man in Spain after the king. On this night the Cardinal had Columbus seated at the place of honor and treated him with ceremonial custom usually reserved for royalty; this meant that every dish served to the Admiral was first tasted by Mendoza, himself, and was then passed, with a cover, to Christopher.

It was also at this auspicious occasion that the oft-repeated "egg incident" was supposed to have taken place. This anecdote is perhaps the best-known tale told about Columbus. As the story goes, during the party a jealous Spanish nobleman, attempting to minimize Christopher's accomplishments, approached the Admiral, and said: "Señor Cristóbal, even if you had not undertaken this great enterprise, we should not have lacked a [Spaniard] who would have made the same discovery that you did" (Morison 2:15).

Columbus said nothing in reply, but instead placed an egg on the table and challenged all the men present to make the egg stand on its end by itself, without the aid of salt, crumbs or any other support. When everyone failed and the egg returned to Christopher, he tapped it on the table slightly crushing one end of the shell, then stood it on the crushed end with no props. The message of this simple demonstration was that when someone shows you how to break beyond self-imposed limits, anyone else can copy the great feat, but it takes a person of vision, courage, and determination to do something that has never before been done (Morison 2:15).

This story was originally printed in *Historia del Mondo Nuovo* (1565), the first Italian history of the New World. The American writer Washington Irving claimed that the "universal popularity of this anecdote is proof of its merit," but others have concluded that the account might be apocryphal (Morison 2:15). Latter-day Saints would be interested to know that Joseph Smith was aware of the story and applied it to himself. In speaking of the insignificance of man's opinions relative to God's wisdom, the Prophet said, "I break the ground; *I lead the way like Columbus* when he was invited to a banquet where he. . . . took an egg and. . . . [illustrated] that when he had once shown the way to the new world nothing was easier than to follow it" (Smith, Joseph 304; emphasis added).

The Second Voyage: Columbus the Christ-bearer

Despite the regal lifestyle he enjoyed while residing at court, the Admiral could no longer stay at Barcelona because the monarchs were anxious for him to embark on another voyage to the New World. Inasmuch as Columbus was at his height of glory, he experienced no difficulty, whatsoever, in financing his second voyage. In fact, his second fleet was much larger than the *Santa Maria*, *Niña*, and *Pinta*, which had set sail in 1492. In 1493 the Admiral commanded 17 vessels, carrying between 1,200 and 1,500 male colonists. He also took a six months' supply of food and provisions. No European nation had ever before ventured to sponsor a colonizing effort of such magnitude (Morison 2:49–50). It was a truly impressive fleet that sailed in 1493 on Columbus' second voyage to the Americas.

The objectives of this second expedition were several: convert the natives; colonize Hispaniola; further explore the Caribbean (in hopes of reaching Asia's mainland); and search for gold. While much has been said of the imperial and financial considerations of the journey, the Admiral's desire to spread Christianity among the natives was one of his preeminent purposes. By starting the process that would eventually lead to the conversion of vast numbers of native Americans, Columbus was, in fact, partially fulfilling yet another Book of Mormon prophecy. Latter-day Saint scholars have always acknowledged Columbus' role in the fulfillment of the familiar prophecy of America's discovery in 1 Nephi 13:12, but have frequently overlooked the vital role he played in fulfilling yet another notable ancient prophecy as he and the Spanish priests who accompanied him on the second voyage were the first Christian missionaries known to have brought the Bible to the inhabitants of the Americas, thus initiating the fulfillment of the prophetic vision given in 1 Nephi 13:38. Nephi, in describing this vision, said: "I beheld the remnant of the seed of my brethren, and also the book of the Lamb of God [the Bible], which had proceeded forth from the mouth of the Jew, that it came forth from the Gentiles unto the remnant of the seed of my brethren."

Evidence that spreading the faith was foremost in Columbus' mind can be found in a letter he wrote to the monarchs prior to the trip, wherein he outlined his recommendations for colonizing Hispaniola. He suggested to the sovereigns "that there be a church [in the new colony] and priests or friars [be sent] for the . . . observance of divine worship and the conversion of the Indians" (Thacher 3:101). The Admiral also suggested "that one per cent of all the gold obtained be taken for the building of the churches and . . . for the maintenance of the priests or friars" (Ibid 105).

Christopher also expressed concern, and rightfully so, that too many colonists would become consumed with searching for gold and hence would soon become derelict in all other responsibilities. He therefore recommended "that the search for gold should be forbidden during some period of the year so that an opportunity be given for the performance of other necessary and profitable labors" (Thacher 3:108). He also suggested "that no

The America That Columbus Encountered

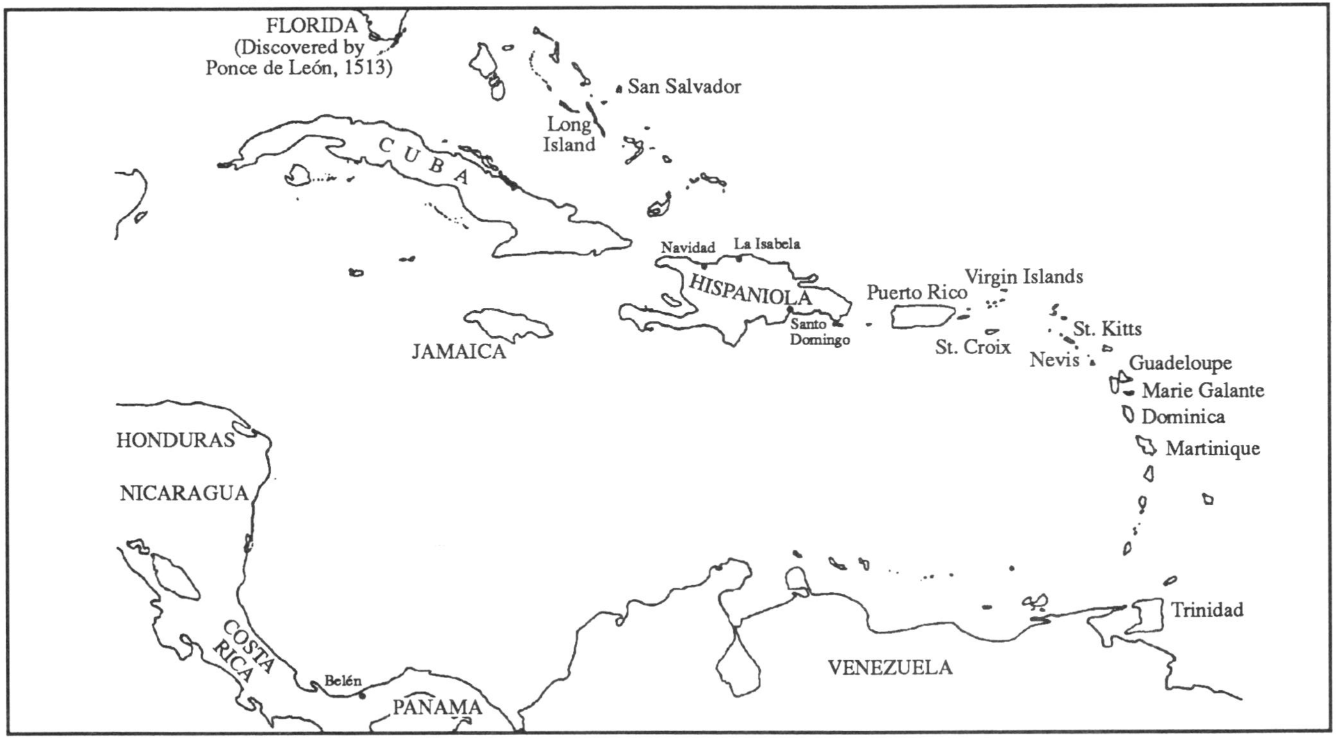

one be allowed the privilege of getting gold except those who settle there and build houses for their dwelling-place in the town" (Ibid 101).

The monarchs' prime interest in this expedition was also of a religious nature, as evidenced by their formal instructions to Christopher, dated 29 May 1493. Acknowledging Columbus' opinion that the natives were "very ripe to be converted," Ferdinand and Isabella directed him "that by all ways and means he strive and endeavor to win over the inhabitants of the said Islands and Mainland to be converted" to Christianity (Morison, *Journals*, 203–04). The crown further commanded Christopher to take with him "the learned father, Fray [Bernardo] Buil, together with [four] other *Religiosos*," for the express purpose that the Indians would be "carefully taught the principles of Our Holy Faith . . . and [that the Admiral himself] provide for their instruction as best he can" (Ibid 204). A further charge from the king and queen concerning the natives was that the Europeans "treat the said Indians very well and lovingly and abstain from doing them any injury, arranging that both peoples hold much conversation and intimacy, each serving the others to the best of their ability" (Ibid.)

The fleet sailed from Cadiz, Spain, on 25 September 1493, stopping briefly at the Canaries, and crossing the ocean in a remarkable 21 days (Morison 2:65). Arriving in the Indies on 3 November, Columbus called all hands to the quarter-deck to offer prayers and sing hymns, "thanking God for His mercy in letting them reach that land" so quickly and safely (Ferdinand 110–11). The Admiral named the site of their first layover after his flagship, the *Mariagalante*. Enroute to Hispaniola, the fleet also passed Dominica, Guadeloupe, Nevis, St. Kitts, St. Croix, the Virgin Islands and Puerto Rico, among others.

When the fleet finally landed at La Navidad, where Columbus had left 39 of his men from the previous voyage, they found ghastly evidence of the fate that had befallen these original settlers. No buildings were visible, and no surviving sailors were to be found. A short search revealed that the Spaniards' fort was now only a charred shell. All the settlers had been killed by neighboring natives, who had rebelled because of mistreatment by the Europeans (Morison 2:91–92).

Saddened but undaunted by this discovery, Columbus abandoned La Navidad and sailed eastward in search of a more suitable place for permanent colonization. Finally, on 2 January 1494, he decided to settle on the northern coast of Hispaniola, in today's Dominican Republic, about 28 miles west of present-day Puerto Plata. Columbus named the site Isabela, which became the first planned European settlement in America (Deagan, "La Isabela," 40–53). Anxious to continue exploring and to find gold in order to justify the expense of this huge expedition, Columbus left this colony in the care of a council headed by his brother, Don Diego, and on 24 April set sail in search of treasure and new lands.

While Christopher was away from Isabela for the next five months, he explored Cuba and discovered the island of Jamaica. When he returned to Isabela on 29 September 1494, he came back to a colonial nightmare (Morison, *Journals,* 404). The Admiral found the island in a state of turmoil, a result of his subordinates' frustration over governing the native Americans as well as the self-serving European settlers, many of whom acted viciously toward the Indians, and maliciously toward their own leaders. Though Columbus may have been the greatest navigator in the world, he was not a very successful governor. He and his brothers could control neither internal rebellion among the settlers nor external fighting with the Indians. Las Casas once said that "the Archangel Gabriel would have been hard put to govern those first colonists of Hispaniola" (Brigham, *Life,* 31). One of the problems was that the Europeans never found enough gold to satisfy their unrealistic expectations. Because of this lack of revenue, the Admiral succumbed to pressure to provide a profitable export to Spain, and therefore consented to the establishment of forced labor and enslavement of native Americans (Morison 2:168–69). This was one of the worst decisions Columbus made in his entire life.

Columbus as Governor: A Turning Point

This decision also seems to have been a turning point in Columbus' career. There is very little evidence in the following few years that he received the same kind of divine guidance and inspiration that he had been so blessed with earlier in his life. During the years he served as governor he appeared to be walking by his own light and stumbled along the way. He made several unfortunate decisions and almost everything seemed to go wrong for him. Modern-day revelation teaches that "the heavens withdraw themselves" when men "exercise unrighteous dominion" over others (D&C 121:37, 39).

Whatever the case, Columbus spent the entire year of 1495 struggling to establish and maintain peace and order on the island of Hispaniola. Then early in 1496 he made plans to return to Spain. By this time he had given up on the idea of establishing Isabela as the main settlement of Hispaniola. Consequently, he gave instructions to his brother, Bartholomew, to look for a new site to serve as the capital of the island and then sailed for Europe on 10 March 1496. While he was gone, Bartholomew founded the city of Santo Domingo on the southeast coast of Hispaniola (Morison 2: 177, 181–82). Within a few years Isabela died out as a colony but Santo Domingo lived on and today owns the distinction of being the oldest European City in the western hemisphere (Pons 2:615).

The Third Voyage: Columbus in Chains

The Admiral's third voyage to the New World took place between 1498 and 1500. This time he commanded a fleet of six ships, and his primary objective was to find a continent and, hopefully, a motherlode of gold. He departed on 30 May and sailed a more southerly course than on his previous voyages. On 13 July the fleet ran into the doldrums and was stalled at sea for eight days, not reaching the Americas until 31 July 1496 (Morison 2:230–43, 246).

The first body of land they sighted was an island that Columbus named Trinidad; however, they did not go ashore at that time. Instead, they sailed through the night and, on 1 August 1498, the Admiral caught his first glimpse of the American mainland, the continent of South America. After sailing through the "Serpent's Mouth," the strait between Trinidad and the continent, Columbus crossed the Gulf of Paria and finally anchored in a harbor on the northeast coast of present-day Venezuela (Morison 2:246–54). When Christopher and his crew went ashore at Venezuela, they became the first Europeans known to history to set foot on the mainland of South America. Columbus would never set foot on the North American continent; the first known European to set foot in what is now the United States was a former shipmate on Columbus' second voyage—Ponce de León went ashore at Florida in 1513 (Ibid 2:56).

It took Columbus a little over three weeks to work his way from Venezuela to Hispaniola, where he anchored on 31 August 1498 at Santo Domingo, the new capital of the island. The Admiral had hoped to rest and recuperate from his difficult voyage when he arrived at Hispaniola; instead, he found the settlement and the island in a state of chaos and rebellion. The Spanish settlers complained that they could not find enough gold, they did not have enough food from Spain, and that the foods indigenous to the Americas were inedible. They also resented the strict rule of the Admiral's brother, Bartholomew, who was, after all, not a Spaniard but a foreigner from Genoa. A man by the name of Francisco Roldán appeared to be the leader of the rebellion (Taviani, *The Great Adventure*, 204–05).

Instead of dealing firmly with the rebels, Columbus, who was tired and sick, tried to pacify them by giving them land grants and allowing them to enslave native Americans. However, many settlers remained discontented and returned to Spain and spread hateful stories about Christopher, accusing him of incompetent leadership (Morison 2:299–301).

In the summer of 1500 the Spanish Monarchs sent Francisco de Bobadilla to Hispaniola to investigate. Bobadilla was given full authority to do whatever he deemed necessary to bring order to the island. An over-zealous government appointee, Bobadilla took full advantage of his new powers on arriving at Hispaniola. He ordered Columbus and his two brothers sent back to Spain in chains to stand trial (Phillips and Phillips 225). Thus, Christopher's third return to Spain contrasted strikingly with the glorious homecoming he experienced after the first voyage, only seven years previous. This third voyage found him in the depths of humiliation and shame, and the experience was definitely a low point in Columbus' life.

The king and queen were shocked when they learned that their Admiral had been humiliated and sent home in shackles. They had Columbus and his brothers released, but they also appointed Nicolás de Ovando to replace Christopher as governor. Ovando sailed to Hispaniola with 30 ships and approximately 2,500 colonists, soldiers, and sailors (Morison 2:310–11, 314). Columbus remained in Spain and began work on his *Book of Prophecies.*

CHAPTER SEVEN

Later Years: the Book of Prophecies and the Final Voyage

> *I pointed out that for the execution of the journey to the Indies I was not aided by intelligence, by mathematics or by maps. It was simply the fulfillment of what Isaiah had prophesied.*
>
> *—Christopher Columbus*

Even though he returned to Spain in chains and was replaced as governor of the New World, Christopher Columbus used the time he had in Spain between his third and fourth voyages to meditate on the events of his life. The circumstances of his latest arrival at court were an obvious contrast to the tremendous rush of fame he had experienced on his first return. Whereas the monarchs had once praised and embraced him, the Spanish crown was now "gracious, but evasive" (Morison 2:311). Having been dismissed from his position as governor of the New World, Columbus set about searching the scriptures and the writings of great philosophers for evidence of his role in the fulfillment of divine destiny. He never published the results of his research, but the manuscript was published in Rome in 1892–94 by Cesare de Lollis as part of an Italian collection of documents entitled *Raccolta di documenti e studi publicati della R. Commissione Colombiana per quarto cen-*

tenario della scoperta dell'America. It was not published in English until in 1991, and interestingly enough, two separate translations appeared that year: *The Libro de las profecías of Christopher Columbus* by Delno C. West and August Kling, and *Christopher Columbus's Book of Prophecies* by Kay Brigham.

Christopher never put a title on his manuscript, but its introductory statement outlined two inter-related purposes for his preparing the work. First, it contained prophecies concerning the final recovery of Jerusalem from Moslem rule and the restoration of the ancient temple (West and Kling 101, 261 n10). Second, it contained passages which prophesied of the discovery and conversion of all "peoples and nations" to Christianity. Other statements in the manuscript make it clear that Columbus believed his own achievements were also a fulfillment of prophecy, and he attempted to place those accomplishments within the framework of divine history, which he believed had a predetermined, unchanging timetable.

The section of the book that gives the most insight into Christopher's thoughts and feelings on these subjects is his introductory letter intended for the Spanish sovereigns. In this letter, the Admiral tried to convince the monarchs to sponsor a crusade to reclaim the Holy Land for Christianity and to restore the temple, an event that he believed was divinely destined to take place.

Columbus substantiated his position by quoting numerous passages from the Old Testament. (I quote the West and Kling and Brigham translations of Columbus' Latin text which occasionally is slightly different from the King James Version.) Isaiah 44:28 reads: "Thou art my shepherd, and thou shalt perform all my pleasure. Who say to Jerusalem: Thou shalt be built. And to the temple: Thy foundations shall be laid" (West and Kling 173). And Isaiah 2:2 reads: "And in the last days the mountain of the house of the Lord shall be prepared on the top of the mountains, and it shall be exalted above the hills: and all nations shall flow unto it" (Ibid 217).

Concerning the theme of the converting all nations to Christianity, Columbus quoted, among others, the following New Testament passages: Matthew 24:14, "And this gospel of the kingdom shall be preached in the whole world, for a testimony to all nations"; Mark 16:15, "Go ye into all the world and preach the gospel to every creature"; and Acts 1:8, "You shall be witnesses unto me in Jerusalem, and in all Judea and Samaria, and even to the uttermost part of the earth" (West and Kling 153). The biblical passage to which Columbus referred most often has also become a Latter-day Saint favorite: John 10:6, "And other sheep I have that are not of this fold: them also I must bring. And they shall hear my voice: and there shall be one fold and one shepherd" (West and Kling 229).

Columbus' understanding of a divine time table for the earth's history gave him a sense of urgency in fulfilling these prophecies. As a result of his studies of Saint Augustine and Pierre d'Ailly, Columbus believed that the earth had a predetermined life span of 7000 years, that all the prophecies in the Bible had to be fulfilled before that time expired, and that "only one hundred and fifty years [remained] for the completion of the seven thousand years which would be the end of the world" (Ibid 109). In short, Columbus believed not only that Jerusalem would be redeemed and that Christianity would be preached to all nations, but he also maintained that these two great events had to be completed in a short period of time.

Perhaps the most intriguing part of the book is where Columbus quoted prophecies from scriptures and learned men that he believed pertained to his own achievements. In his introductory letter to the Spanish monarchs, Columbus stated that the Enterprise of the Indies "all turned out just as our redeemer Jesus Christ had said, and as he had spoken earlier by the mouth of his holy prophets" (West and Kling 107). A little later in the letter, Christopher again declared that "the execution of the journey to the Indies. . . . was simply the fulfillment of what Isaiah had prophesied" (Ibid 111).

Columbus does not specify which of Isaiah's prophecies he had in mind, but among the more than two dozen listed was Isaiah 42:1–4: "Behold my servant: I will uphold him. My elect: my soul lighteth in him. I have given my spirit upon him. . . . and the islands shall wait for his law" (West and Kling 171). Another passage was Isaiah 55:5: "Behold thou shalt call a nation which thou knewest not: and the nations that knew not thee shall run to thee, because of the Lord thy God, and for the Holy One of Israel; for he glorified thee" (Ibid 169). He also quoted several passages from Psalms that seem to point to his own life: Psalms 2:8, "Ask of me and I will make nations your inheritance, and the ends of the earth your possession"; and 18:43–44: "You have made me the head of nations; people I did not know are subject to me. . . . Therefore I will praise you among the nations, O Lord" (Brigham, *Book of Prophecies*, 184–85).

In addition to quoting passages in the Bible, Columbus also quoted nonscriptural writings that he believed pertained to his Enterprise to the Indies. One of the most fascinating of these was Seneca's tragedy *Medea*, which predicted that "In the latter years of the world will come certain times in which the Ocean Sea will relax the bonds of things, and a great land will open up, and a new mariner like the one who was the guide of Jason, whose name was Typhis, will discover a new world" (West and Kling 227). The Admiral's son, Ferdinand, also quoted this passage in his biography of Columbus, and added, "Now it is considered certain that this prophecy was fulfilled in the person of the Admiral" (Ferdinand 18).

Notwithstanding his belief that such great prophecies pertained to his life and to his discovery of the New World, Columbus was simultaneously humbled by his search of the scriptures. This fact is demonstrated by one of his final remarks in his introductory letter to Ferdinand and Isabella. In a candid assessment of his spiritual condition, Christopher confessed: "*I am only a most unworthy sinner*, but ever since I have cried out for grace and mercy from the Lord, they have covered me completely" (West and Kling 111; emphasis added).

It seems obvious that preparing the *Book of Prophecies* had given Columbus significant opportunity to ponder his spiritual well-being and standing before the Lord. With the benefit of such a period of introspection and study, Christopher felt himself again prepared to brave the seas and travel to the New World.

The Fourth Voyage: A Call to Repentance

Commanding a fleet of four ships and 140 men, Columbus set sail for America for the fourth and final time on 9 May 1502 (Morison 2:319–22). The Admiral's son and future biographer, Ferdinand, was one of the crew members of the expedition. The objective of this voyage was to discover a passage through the recently discovered American continent to the Indian Ocean (Lemos 2:720). On his way to explore the American coast, Columbus made landfall at Martinique, then continued on, making history as he discovered present-day Honduras, Nicaragua, Costa Rica and Panama (Morison, *Journals*, 406–07).

In the midst of his exploration of the coast of Panama, Columbus anchored the fleet on 6 January 1503 at the mouth of a river he named Belén. He decided to remain in the area at least until the end of the rainy season, and sent patrols to search for gold. Upon discovering entire "mines of gold," the Admiral decided to establish a settlement at Belén; Christopher would leave his brother, Bartholomew, in charge while he returned to Spain. The men set out in February to establish the settlement on the river shore, but their efforts were soon interrupted by aggressive natives, who hoped to kill the intruders (Morison 2:366–71).

On 6 April, the day that Christopher was to sail for Spain, the majority of his party accompanied the Admiral to his ships to bid farewell, leaving only 20 men and a dog on the shore.

With a large numerical advantage, 400 heavily armed natives descended on the small guard party, killing one and wounding several, including Bartholomew. In the meantime, ignorant of the attack, Columbus sent a group of men ashore to take on a final load of water for the return voyage. The men of this party walked right into the Indians' hands, and all but one of this company were killed (Morison 2:372–73).

During the fight, the Admiral was left alone aboard his ship, the *Capitana*, which was anchored about a mile off shore. Physically sick and, no doubt, greatly distressed over the plight of his men, Columbus climbed to the top of the vessel and tried desperately to attract the attention of his war captains. After calling, unsuccessfully, for his men, he eventually succumbed to exhaustion and fell asleep (Ibid 373–74).

Slumbering aboard the *Capitana*, Christopher had perhaps the most remarkable, and sobering, spiritual experience of his life. He "heard a compassionate voice," calling him to repentance:

> O fool, and slow to believe and serve thy God, the God of every Man! What more did He do for Moses or for David His servant than for thee? From thy birth He hath ever held thee in special charge. When He saw thee at man's estate, marvelously did He cause thy name to resound over the earth. The Indies, so rich a portion of the world, He gave thee for thine own, and thou hast divided them as it pleased thee. Of those barriers of the Ocean Sea, which were closed with such mighty chains, He hath given thee the keys. . . . Thou hast won noble fame from Christendom. . . . Turn thou to Him and acknowledge thy faults; His mercy is infinite. (Morison, *Journals*, 378)

Columbus, obviously humbled by this admonition, said that he had "no answer to give in definite words," leaving him only "to weep for [his] transgressions." The final words spoken by the voice gave Christopher a feeling of hope and comfort: "Fear not, but have trust" (Ibid).

This incident was, in fact, a moving call to repentance for the Admiral. The records of his earlier life make clear that Christopher had a keen spiritual sense about him; his expressions of faith and gratitude to the Lord were both impressive and numerous. However, from the time that he assumed the trying duties of governor of the Indies during his second voyage (1494) until this climactic call to repentance during the fourth voyage (1503), his life seemed little directed by spiritual influence. The impact of this experience seems to have directed Christopher back to the level of spiritual awareness and devotion that he had enjoyed earlier in his life.

With these poignant thoughts to ponder, the Admiral returned to Spain in November 1504 to live out the last year-and-a-half of his illustrious, yet turbulent, life. He died in Valladolid, Castile, on Wednesday, 20 May 1506. His last words were "'*in manus tuas, Domine, commendo spiritum meum*' ('into your hands, O Lord, I commend my spirit')" (Taviani, *The Great Adventure*, 248).

Epilogue

For Latter-day Saints, the story of Christopher Columbus does not begin with his birth in 1451; nor does it end with his death in 1506. Because they believe that everyone associated with this earth lived as spirit children of our Heavenly Father in a premortal state before they came to earth, they believe that Columbus lived before he came here. And because they believe that life continues after death, they believe he is now in the Spirit World awaiting the resurrection with millions of other spirits who have passed from this life.

But Latter-day Saints are more involved in Columbus' life than just believing that he lived in a premortal state and waiting for him to be resurrected. They believe that he was an instrument in the Lord's hand to discover the Americas to the Europeans. That in turn brought the Founding fathers here to establish the United States of America. Its freedoms made it possible to restore the Church of Jesus Christ to the earth. And there is still more.

They have a tradition that President Wilford Woodruff, while he was serving as the President of the St. George Temple, was visited by the spirits of several great men who requested him to perform vicarious baptism for them in the temple. Speaking of that experience, President Woodruff said:

> the spirits of the dead gathered around me, wanting to know why we did not redeem them. Said they, "You have had the use of the Endowment House for a number of years, and yet nothing has ever been done for us. We laid the foundation of the government you now enjoy, and we never apostatized from it, but we remained true to it and were faithful to God." These were the signers of the Declaration of Independence, and they waited on me for two days and two nights. I thought it very singular , that notwithstanding so much work had been done, and yet nothing had been done for them. The thought never entered my heart, from the fact, I suppose, that heretofore our minds were reaching after our more immediate friends and relatives. I straightway went into

> the baptismal font [in the temple] and called upon brother McCallister to baptize me for the signers of the Declaration of Independence, and fifty other eminent men, making one hundred in all, including John Wesley, Columbus, and others. (*JD* 19:229)

On the same day these ordinances were performed, President Woodruff records in his journal that he baptized brother McCallister "for 21, including Gen Washington & his forefathers and all the Presidents of the United States that were on my list except Buchanan Van Buren & Grant. . . . Sister Lucy Bigelow Young went forth into the font and was Baptized for Martha Washington and her family and seventy (70) of the Eminent women of the world. . . . There were Baptized in all to day 682" (Woodruff, *Journal* 7:367–69). All these proxy ordinances are performed for the dead so they as spirits in the Spirit World may accept or reject them.

As President Ezra Taft Benson presided over the Church in 1992, the 500th anniversary of Columbus' epic voyage, it seems appropriate to quote his appraisal of the man and the other "eminent men" whose temple ordinances were performed by President Woodruff:

> The temple work for the fifty-six signers of the Declaration of Independence and other founding fathers has been done. All these appeared to Wilford Woodruff when he was President of the St. George Temple. President George Washington was ordained a High Priest at that time. You will also be interested to know that according to Wilford Woodruff's journal, John Wesley, Benjamin Franklin, and Christopher Columbus were also ordained High Priests at the time. When one casts doubt upon the character of these noble sons of God, I believe he or she will have to answer to the God of heaven for it. (Benson 604)

Notwithstanding the mistakes he made in his life and the human faults he had, Christopher Columbus was a man of notable spiritual sensitivity. Given the powers of repentance and forgiveness, it should come as no surprise that President Wilford Woodruff vicariously had his endowments done and ordained him a High Priest three days after he was baptized for him.

APPENDIX A

Statements by Modern-Day Prophets and Apostles on Columbus

Joseph Smith

I lead the way like Columbus when he was invited to a banquet where he was assigned the most honorable place at the table, and served with the ceremonials which were observed towards sovereigns. A shallow courtier present, who was meanly jealous of him, abruptly asked him whether he thought that in case he had not discovered the Indies, there were not other men in Spain who would have been capable of the enterprise? Columbus made no reply, but took an egg and invited the company to make it stand on end. They all attempted it, but in vain; whereupon he struck it upon the table so as to break one end, and left it standing on the broken part, illustrating that when he had once shown the way to the new world nothing was easier than to follow it. (*Teachings of the Prophet Joseph Smith* 304)

Brigham Young

The Almighty . . . moved upon Columbus to launch forth upon the trackless deep to discover the American Continent; he moved upon the signers of the Declaration of Independence; and he moved upon Washington to fight and conquer, in the same way as he moved upon ancient and modern Prophets, each being inspired to accomplish the particular work he was called to perform in the times, seasons, and dispensations of the Almighty. God's purpose, in raising up these men and inspiring them with daring sufficient to surmount every opposing power, was to prepare the way for the formation of a true Republican government. (*JD* 7:13)

Parley P. Pratt

Hence we contemplate that small beginning made by the American pioneers, by Columbus, the first pioneer, and by our fathers the pioneers of religion and liberty; we contemplate how that influence has spread and increased in the earth, influencing the feelings of individuals as well as national institutions . . . until by and by the rest of the world is overwhelmed, that it is obliged to bow to their superior greatness. (*JD* 1:43)

Orson Pratt

Some of [the religious reformers] were wrought upon to come to this continent for the purpose of securing to themselves religious freedom and religious right; and inspired by the Almighty, as was Columbus, who discovered this land, they planted their feet upon the American soil. (*JD* 3:72)

While the iron hand of despotism thus held the nations within its withering grasp, enslaving both body and soul, the great God, near the close of the fifteenth century, moved upon the mind of a Columbus, and inspired him to fearlessly launch forth upon the great expanse of unknown waters on the west of Europe; and guided by the invisible agency of the Holy Spirit, he revealed to the down trodden, despairing nations, a new world. (*JD* 7:214)

John Taylor

Could we have been placed in any better position than we are today? No. What has been the object of God for sometime? In the first place He operated upon Columbus to come and find this land. (*JD* 23:19)

Wilford Woodruff

I straightway went into the baptismal font and called upon brother McCallister to baptize me for the signers of the Declaration of Independence, and fifty other eminent men, making one hundred in all, including John Wesley, Columbus, and others. (*JD* 19:229)

Columbus was inspired of God to persevere as he did to discover this continent, and thus prepare the way for a class of people upon whom the Spirit of the Lord moved to follow. (*JD* 23:82)

When Columbus was moved upon by the Spirit of God, to cross the ocean to find a new continent, his object and desires were unpopular with those by whom he was surrounded. (*JD* 24:4)

George Q. Cannon

Columbus was inspired to penetrate the ocean and discover this Western continent, for the set time for its discovery had come, and the consequences which God desired to follow its discovery have taken place—a free government has been established on it. The men who established that Government were inspired of God—George Washington, Thomas Jefferson, John Adams, Benjamin Franklin, and all the fathers of the Republic were inspired to do the work which they did. We believe it was a preparatory work for the establishment of the kingdom of God. This Church and kingdom could not have been established on the earth if their work had not been performed. (*JD* 14: 55)

This land was kept secret until Columbus was moved upon by the Spirit of God, to go forth and penetrate the western ocean. Then the land was settled and a government was formed under the protecting aegis of liberty, and a place was found for the establishment of the Kingdom of God. (*JD* 21:201)

This land was kept for this purpose. For centuries it was hidden from all the nations of the earth. It was not until the 15th century that God inspired Columbus to go forth and seek a passage across the Atlantic, and land upon some of the islands adjacent to this continent. His track was followed by other. (*JD* 23:103)

Orson Hyde

This same angel [Moroni] presides over the destinies of America, and feels a lively interest in all our doings. He was in the camp of Washington; and by an invisible hand, led on our fathers to conquest and victory; and all this to open and prepare the way for the Church and kingdom of God to be established on the western hemisphere, for the redemption of Israel and the salvation of the world. This same angel was with Columbus, and gave him deep impressions, by dreams and by visions, respecting this New World. Trammelled by poverty and by an unpopular cause, yet his persevering and unyielding heart would not allow any obstacle in his way too great for him to overcome; and the angel of God helped him—was with him on the stormy deep, calmed the troubled elements, and guided his frail vessel to the desired haven. Under the guardianship of this same angel, or Prince of America, have the United States grown, increased, and flourished, like the sturdy oak by the rivers of water. (*JD* 6:368)

Observe Christopher Columbus in his silent meditations; mark his untiring and faithful observations! Behold him watching the western breeze, and marking, with zealous eye and anxious heart, every substance that floated on the ocean's eastward bound current. . . . Inspired of the Almighty God of Heaven, he encountered the ridicule and jeer of a faithless and unbelieving world. . . . The Spirit Angel was their guardian and their guide, and was with them on the stormy deep. (*JD* 7:107–08)

Compare the coming of the Saints here, with the banishment of Joseph into Egypt, and the manner in which Columbus was sent off on his perilous exploration, and note the conclusion that follows. The world dreaded the germs of greatness which they saw. (*JD* 10:376)

There must needs be opposition in all things. We are told that in 1492 this American continent was discovered by Christopher Columbus. Look at the exertions made by him to obtain the necessary means to effect the discovery. It required ships, means and men to enable him to make his way across the trackless deep. . . . The Spirit of God came upon him and he had no rest day or night until he accomplished what the Spirit wrought upon him to do. . . . He applied to different crowned heads, and received rebuffs and discouragements. He was poor; the plans of Jehovah are mostly carried out by humble and poor individuals. So it was with Columbus; he was poor, but daring and persevering, and with a soul formed within his bosom to understand and prosecute the great enterprise that was to bring to light a vast continent reserved in the providence of God. (*JD* 10:375)

Joseph F. Smith

Christ taught the gospel to Adam, and made known his truths to Abraham and the prophets. He was the inspirer of the ancient philosophers, Pagan or Israelite, as well as of the great characters of modern times. Columbus, in discovery; Washington, in the struggle for freedom; Lincoln, in emancipation and union; Bacon, in philosophy; Franklin, in statesmanship and diplomacy; Stephenson, in steam; Watts, in song; Edison, in electricity, and Joseph Smith, in theology and religion, found in Christ the source of their wisdom and the marvelous truths which they advocated. (*Gospel Doctrine* 31)

Orson F. Whitney

We believe . . . that Joseph Smith was inspired to begin this work, just as Gallileo [sic], Columbus, and other mighty men of old, whom I have not mentioned, were inspired to gradually pave the way leading to this dispensation. (*JD* 24:201)

John A. Widtsoe

The world owes most to the men, great and small, who in the name of truth have dared to challenge tradition. . . . In the public square of Genoa, 120 miles north of Pisa, stands a heroic monument to Christopher Columbus, one of the finest in Europe. Columbus spent the years of his young manhood in Genoa, and dreamed his great dreams there. A few miles northward, a little village puffs and blows because in it Columbus was born. Yet, when he challenged the geographical tradition of his day, he was scorned by his compatriots; and even when he had discovered America, jealousy and misunderstanding landed him in prison and left him broken-hearted. Nevertheless, the great era of geographical exploration and discovery may well be dated from Columbus. The history of human progress is indeed but the story of the men who have loved truth above all else, and who have refused to be coerced by unsupported tradition, however powerful its advocates have been. (*Man and the Dragon* 67–69)

Mark E. Petersen

The vision [1 Nephi 13:12] then became more specific. Says Nephi:

> And I looked and beheld a man among the Gentiles, who was separated from the seed of my brethren by the many waters; and I beheld the Spirit of God, that it came down and wrought upon the man; and he went forth upon the many waters; even unto the seed of my brethren who were in the promised land.

It was Christopher Columbus whom he saw, and he observed that the discoverer was guided by divine power on his journey. (*The Great Prologue* 3)

Spencer W. Kimball

Columbus was led by God. I'm sure that he inspired a little boy, Christopher Columbus, to stand on the quays in Genoa, Italy, and yearn for the sea. He was filled with the desire to sail the seas, and he fulfilled a great prophecy made long, long ago that this land, chosen above all other lands, should be discovered. And so when he was mature, opportunity was granted to him to brave the unknown seas, to find this land which had been cut off from the rest of the world long centuries, and to open the door, as it were. (*Teachings of Spencer W. Kimball* 427)

Ezra Taft Benson

God inspired "a man among the Gentiles" (1 Nephi 13:12) who, by the Spirit of God was led to rediscover the land of America and bring this rich new land to the attention of the people in Europe. That man, of course, was Christopher Columbus, who testified that he was inspired in what he did. (*Teachings of Ezra Taft Benson* 577)

The temple work for the fifty-six signers of the Declaration of Independence and other founding fathers has been done. All these appeared to Wilford Woodruff when he was President of the St. George Temple. President George Washington was ordained a High Priest at that time. You will also be interested to know that according to Wilford Woodruff's journal, John Wesley, Benjamin Franklin, and Christopher Columbus were also ordained High Priests at the time. When one casts doubt about the character of these noble sons of God, I believe he or she will have to answer to God for it. (*Ibid* 604)

APPENDIX B

Statements by Columbus with Spiritual Significance

I have had business and conversation with learned men among both laity and clergy, Latins and Greeks, Jews and Moslems, and many others of different religions. I prayed to the most merciful Lord concerning my desire, and he gave me the spirit and the intelligence for it. . . .

During this time, I have searched out and studied all kinds of texts: geographies, histories, chronologies, philosphies and other subjects. With a hand that could be felt, the Lord opened my mind to the fact that it would be possible to sail from here to the Indies, and he opened my will to desire to accomplish the project. . . .

Who can doubt that this fire was not merely mine, but also of the Holy Spirit who encouraged me with a radiance of marvelous illumination from his sacred Holy Scriptures, by a most clear and powerful testimony . . . urging me to press forward? Continually, without a moment's hesitation, the Scriptures urge me to press forward with great haste. (West and Kling, *Libro de las profecías*, 105)

* * * * *

The Lord purposed that there should be something clearly miraculous in this matter of the voyage to the Indies, so as to encourage me and others in the other matter of the Household of God. I spent seven years here in your royal court discussing this subject with the leading persons in all the learned arts, and their conclusion was that all was in vain. That was the end, and they gave it up. But afterwards it all turned out just as our redeemer Jesus Christ had said, and as he had spoken earlier by the mouth of his holy prophets. . . .

And I lay aside all the sciences and books that I indicated above. I hold only to the sacred Holy Scriptures, and to the interpretations of prophecy by certain devout persons who have spoken on this subject by divine illumination. . . .

I believe that the Holy Spirit works among Christians, Jews and Moslems, and among all men of every faith, not merely among the learned, but also among the uneducated. (West and Kling 107)

* * * * *

Already I pointed out that for the execution of the journey to the Indies I was not aided by intelligence, by mathematics or my maps. It was simply the fulfillment of what Isaiah had prophesied. (Ibid 111)

* * * * *

I feel persuaded, by the many and wonderful manifestations of Divine Providence in my especial favour, that I am the chosen instrument of God in bringing to pass a great event—no less than the conversion of millions who are now existing in the darkness of Paganism.

(Lester, *The Life and Voyages of Americus Vespucius* 79)

I fell asleep, and heard a compassionate voice, saying, "O fool, and slow to believe and serve thy God, the God of every man! What more did He do for Moses or for David His servant than for thee? From thy birth He hath ever held thee in special charge. When He saw thee at man's estate, marvelously did He cause thy name to resound over the earth. The Indies, so rich a portion of the world, He gave thee for thine own, and thou hast divided them as it pleased thee. Of those barriers of the Ocean Sea, which were closed with such mighty chains, He hath given thee the keys. Thou was obeyed in so many lands, and thou has won noble fame from Christendom. What more did he do for the people of Israel, when He carried them out of Egypt; or for David, whom from a shepherd He raised to be king over Judea? Turn thou to Him and acknowledge thy faults; His mercy is infinite; . . . I heard all this as in a swoon, but I had no answer to give in definite words; so true, only to weep for my transgression. (Morison, *Journals*, 378)

* * * * *

In the name of the most Holy Trinity, who inspired me with the idea and afterward made it perfectly clear to me, that I could navigate and go to the Indies from Spain, by traversing the ocean westwardly. (Curtis, *The Authentic Letters of Columbus*, 193)

* * * * *

Our Lord made me the messenger of the new heaven and the new earth, of which he spoke in the Book of Revelation by St. John, after having spoken of it by the mouth of Isaiah; *and he showed me the place where to find it.* (Brigham, *Life,* 50, 57n; emphasis added)

APPENDIX C

One Hundred Eminent Men Baptized by Proxy in the St. George Temple, 21 August 1877

A. Signers of the Declaration of Independence (except John Hancock and William Floyd). [Alphabetized for ease of reference. *Ordained High Priests by Proxy August 22–24.]

John Adams
Samuel Adams
Josiah Bartlett
Carter Braxton
Charles Carroll of Carrolton
Samuel Chase
Abraham Clark
George Clymer
William Ellery
*Benjamin Franklin
Elbridge Gerry
Button Gwinnett
Lyman Hall
Benjamin Harrison
Joseph Hewes
William Hooper
Stephen Hopkins
Samuel Huntington
Thomas Jefferson
Thomas Nelson Jr
Thomas Heywood Jr
Thomas Lynch Jr
Francis Lightfoot Lee
Richard Henry Lee
Francis Lewis
Philip Livingston
Thomas McKean
Lewis Morris
Robert Morris
John Morton
Arthur Myddleton
William Chase Paca
Robert Treat Paine
John Penn
George Read
Caezer Rodney
George Ross
Benjamin Rush
Edward Rutledge
Roger Sherman

James Smith
Thomas Stone
George Taylor
Matthew Thornton
George Walton
William Whipple
William Williams
James Wilson
Oliver Wolcott
George Wythe

B. Baptized for the following Eminent Men:

Lewis John Rudolph Agassis
Charles Louis Napolean Bonapart
Lord Henry Brougham
Edward George Earl Lytton Bulwer
Robert Burns
Lord George Gordon Byron
John Calwell Cahoon
Count Camillo Bonso di Cavour
Thomas Chalmers
Henry Clay
Richard Cobden
*Christopher Columbus
Daniel O Connell
John Filpot Corran
Michael Faraday
David Glascoe Farragut
David Garrick
Edward Gibbon
Johann Wolfgang Goethe
Oliver Goldsmith
Henry Grattan
Washington Irving
Thomas Johnathan Jackson
Samuel Johnson
Benito Juarez
John Philip Kemple
Baron Justus von Liebig
David Livingstone
Thomas Babington Macauley
Lord Horatio Nelson
George Peobody
Frederick 2d king of Prussia
Count Demetrius Perepa
Hiram Powers
Sir Joshua Reynolds
Frederick Von Schiller
Sir Walter Scott
William Henry Seward
George Stephenson
William Makepeace Thackerey
Americus Vespucius
Frederick Henry Alexander Von Humbolt
Daniel Webster
*John Wesley
William Wordsworth

Source: *Wilford Woodruff s Journal* 7:367-368.

APPENDIX D

Chronology of Christopher Columbus' Life

c. 600 BC ..... Nephi prophesies of Columbus's journey.
AD 1451 ...... Columbus born in Genoa, between 25 August and 31 October.
c. 1471 .... Voyage to Tunis.
1474-75 .... One or two voyages to Chios.
1476 .... Moves to Portugal.
1477 .... Voyage to Iceland.
1478-79 .... Voyage to Madeira Islands.
1479 .... Marriage to Doña Felipa Perestrello e Moniz.
1480 .... First son, Diego, born at Porto Santo.
1480-81 .... Correspondence with Paolo Toscanelli of Florence.
1482-84 .... At least one voyage to the Gold Coast of Africa.
1484-85 .... Proposes "Enterprise of the Indies" to King John II of Portugal. Doña Felipa dies.
1485 .... Moves to Spain.
1486 .... First proposal to Spanish crown; Enterprise is rejected.
1487 .... Placed on Spanish royal payroll.
1488 .... Removed from Spanish payroll. Columbus accepts King John's invitation to return to Portugal. Second son, Ferdinand, is born.
1489 .... Second proposal upon returning to Spain.
1490 .... Second proposal rejected.
1491 .... Third proposal to Spanish sovereigns.

1492

January .... Third proposal rejected; Santangel intercedes, Queen agrees to sponsor Enterprise.

FIRST VOYAGE

3 August ...... Departs Palos, Spain, with three ships.
12 August ..... Arrives at Canary Islands.
6 September ... Begins ocean passage, course due west.
9 September ... Leaves sight of land.
23 September .. Sea rises "without wind."
7 October ..... Course changed to west-southwest.
10 October .... Crew threatens mutiny.
11 October .... Course changed back to due west.
12 October .... Land sighted at San Salvador.
28 October .... Lands at Cuba.
6 December .... Arrives at Hispaniola.
24 December ... *Santa María* runs aground at La Navidad.
26 December .. Construction of fort begins at La Navidad.

1493

16 January ..... Fleet sails for Spain.
12 February .... Violent storm arises.
14 February .... *Niña* and *Pinta* separated in gale.
15 February .... *Niña* sights Azores.
4 March ...... Columbus arrives at Lisbon, Portugal.
15 March ...... Arrives at Palos, Spain.

SECOND VOYAGE

25 September .. Fleet of 17 ships sails from Cadiz, Spain.
3 November ... Landfall at Dominica; Columbus anchors at Mariagalante.

4-19 November Passes Guadeloupe, Nevis, St. Kitts, St. Croix, Virgin Islands and Puerto Rico.

27 November . . Arrives at La Navidad; finds settlement destroyed.

1494

2 January . . . . . . Arrives at Isabela; founds city.

24 April–29 September . . . . Explores Caribbean.

1495

Columbus spends entire year struggling to maintain peace and order on Hispaniola. Consents to the enslavement of Caribbean natives.

1496

10 March. . . . . . . Columbus departs for Spain.

11 June . . . . Arrives at Cadiz, Spain.

c. 1497

Under Admiral's direction, Santo Domingo founded by Bartholomew Columbus while Christopher is in Spain.

1498

THIRD VOYAGE

30 May . . . . Departs Spain for New World with six ships.

13-22 July . . . . . Fleet stalled in Doldrums.

31 July . . . . Landfall at Trinidad.

1 August . . . . . . First sighting of South America (Venezuela).

6 August . . . . . . Lands on South American mainland, and takes possession of Venezuela.

31 August ..... Anchors off Hispaniola.
October .... Francisco Roldán leads rebellion in Hispaniola.

1499

September .... Columbus makes temporary peace with rebels.

1500

23 August ..... Francisco de Bobadilla lands at Santo Domingo, arrests Columbus and his brothers.
early October .. Columbus sent to Spain as a prisoner in chains.
late October ... Arrives Cadiz, Spain.
12 December ... Monarchs order Columbus released; summon him to court.
17 December ... Audience with Monarchs at Alhambra, Spain.

1501

3 September ... Nicolas de Ovando named new governor of Hispaniola.

1502

13 February .... Ovando sails for New World with 30 ships.
February ...... Christopher remains in Spain to work on Book of Prophecies.

FOURTH VOYAGE

9 May .... Columbus sets sail from Cadiz, Spain, for Americas with four ships.
15 June .... Landfall at Martinique.
30 July–5 October
.... Explores Central America; discovers Honduras, Nicaragua, Costa Rica and Panama.

1503

6 January . . . . . . Anchors off coast of Panama at Río Belén.
6 April . . . . Battle of Belén. Columbus hears "compassionate voice" call him to repentance.

1504

12 September . . Columbus departs for Spain.
7 November . . . Arrives Sanlúcar, Spain.

1506

20 May . . . . Dies at Valladolid, Spain.

1830

Nephi's prophecy of Columbus is published in Book of Mormon.

1877

21 August . . . . . Wilford Woodruff was baptized vicariously for Christopher Columbus in the St. George Temple.
24 August . . . . . Christopher Columbus was vicariously endowed and ordained a High Priest in the St. George Temple.

Bibliography

Anghera, Peter Martyr, d'. *De Orbe Novo*. 2 Vols. Trans. Francis Augustus MacNutt. New York: G. P. Putnam's Sons, The Knickerbocker Press, 1912.

Backman, Milton V. *Myths and Realities of Colonial American History*. Provo, UT: Brigham Young University, Extension Publications, 1966.

Bedini, Silvio A. "Signature." *The Christopher Columbus Encyclopedia*. 2 Vols. Ed. Silvio A. Bedini. New York: Simon & Schuster, 1992. 2:62830.

Benson, Ezra Taft. *The Teachings of Ezra Taft Benson*. Salt Lake City: Bookcraft, 1988.

Brigham, Kay. *Christopher Columbus: His Life and Discovery in the Light of His Prophecies*. Barcelona: CLIE, 1990.

———. *Christopher Columbus's Book of Prophecies*. Barcelona: CLIE, 1991.

Carlinsky, Dan. "Christopher Confusion." *Modern Maturity* (Feb-Mar 1992) 35:50-55.

Cheesman, Paul R. *The World of the Book of Mormon*. Salt Lake City: Deseret Book Company, 1978.

Christopher Columbus Encyclopedia, The. 2 Vols. Ed. Silvio A. Bedini. New York: Simon & Schuster, 1992.

Colón, Cristóbal. *Textos y documentos completos Relaciones de viajes, cartas y memoriales*. Ed. Consuelo Varela. Madrid: Alianza, 1982.

Columbus, Ferdinand. *The Life of the Admiral Christopher Columbus by His Son Ferdinand*. Trans. Benjamin Keen. New Brunswick, NJ: Rutgers University Press, 1959.

Curtis, William E. *The Authentic Letters of Columbus.* Chicago: Field Columbian Museum, 1895.

Deagan, Kathleen. "La Isabela: Europe's First Foothold in the New World." *National Geographic* (Jan 1992) 181:4053.

———. "Settlements: La Isabela." *The Christopher Columbus Encyclopedia.* 2 Vols. Ed. Silvio A. Bedini. New York: Simon & Schuster, 1992. 2:608-10.

Dunn, Oliver and James E. Kelley, Jr. *The Diario of Christopher Columbus' First Voyage to America, 1492-1493.* Norman, OK: University of Oklahoma Press, 1989.

Earenfight, Theresa. "João II." *The Christopher Columbus Encyclopedia.* 2 Vols. Ed. Silvio A. Bedini. New York: Simon & Schuster, 1992. 1:396-97.

Fernández-Armesto, Felipe. *Columbus: And the Conquest of the Impossible.* London: Weidenfeld and Nicolson, 1974.

Flinders, Neil J. "Christopher Columbus: 'The Spirit of God . . . Wrought Upon the Man.'" Unpublished manuscript.

Fuson, Robert H. *The Log of Christopher Columbus.* Camden, Me: International Marine Publishing, 1992.

Grover, Mark L. *Columbus: A Selective Bibliography of the Brigham Young University Library.* Provo, UT: Brigham Young University, Harold B. Lee Library, 1992.

Hanson, Louise G. "Columbus, Christopher." *Encyclopedia of Mormonism.* 5 Vols. New York: Macmillan Publishing Company, 1992. 1:294-96.

Jones, W. R. "Polo, Marco." *The Christopher Columbus Encyclopedia.* 2 Vols. Ed. Silvio A. Bedini. New York: Simon & Schuster, 1992. 2:556-58.

Journal of Discourses. 26 vols. 1854-86.

Kimball, Spencer W. *The Teachings of Spencer W. Kimball.* Ed. Edward L. Kimball. Salt Lake City: Bookcraft, 1982.

Las Casas, Bartolomé de. *History of the Indies.* Trans. and Ed. Andree Collard. Ed. Silvio A. Bedini. New York: Harper & Row, 1971.

Lemos, William. "Voyages of Columbus." *The Christopher Columbus Encyclopedia.* 2 Vols. Ed. Silvio A. Bedini. New York: Simon & Schuster, 1992. 2:693-728.

Lester, C. Edwards. *The Life and Voyages of Americus Vespucius.* New York: New Amsterdam Book Company, 1903.

Lollis, Cesare de. Ed. *Raccolta di documenti e studi publicati della R. Commissione Colombiana per quarto centerario della scoperta dell'America.* 6 multivolume Parts. Roma 1894.

Lyon, Eugene. "Search for Columbus." *National Geographic* (Jan 1992) 181:2-39.

McKay, John P., Bennett D. Hill, and John Buckler. *A History of World Societies.* Boston: Houghton Mifflin Company, 1988.

Merrill, Hyde M. "Christopher Columbus & The Book of Mormon." *The Improvement Era* (Feb 1966) 69:97-98, 135-36.

Morison, Samuel Eliot. *Admiral of the Ocean Sea.* 2 Vols. Boston: Little, Brown and Co., 1942.

———. *Journals and Other Documents on the Life and Voyages of Christopher Columbus.* New York: The Heritage Press, 1963.

Nader, Helen. "Columbus, Christopher: Adolescence and Youth." *The Christopher Columbus Encyclopedia.* 2 Vols. Ed. Silvio A. Bedini. New York: Simon & Schuster, 1992. 1:163-67.

Newsweek: Columbus Special Issue. Fall/Winter 1991.

Nibley, Hugh. "Columbus and Revelation." *The Instructor* (Oct 1953) 88:319-20.

Nunn, George E. *The Geographical Conceptions of Columbus.* New York: American Geographical Society, 1924.

Palmer, Spencer J. *Mormons and Muslims.* Provo, UT: Religious Studies Center, 1983.

Petersen, Mark E. *The Great Prologue.* Salt Lake City: Deseret Book Co., 1975.

Phillips, William D., Jr., and Carla Rahn Phillips. *The Worlds of Christopher Columbus.* Cambridge: Cambridge University Press, 1992.

Pons, Frank Moya. "Settlements: Santo Domingo." *The Christopher Columbus Encyclopedia.* 2 Vols. Ed. Silvio A. Bedini. New York: Simon & Schuster, 1992. 2:615-16.

Provost, Foster. *Columbus Dictionary.* Detroit: Omnigraphics, Inc., 1991.

Roberts, B.H. *Defense of the Faith and the Saints.* Salt Lake City: The Deseret News, 1907.

Russell, Jeffrey Burton. *Inventing the Flat Earth: Columbus and Modern Historians.* New York: Praeger, 1991.

Smith, Joseph. *Teachings of the Prophet Joseph Smith.* Comp. Joseph Fielding Smith. Salt Lake City: Deseret Book Co., 1963.

Smith, Joseph F. *Gospel Doctrine.* Salt Lake City: Deseret Book Co., 1977.

Taviani, Paolo Emilio. *Christopher Columbus: The Grand Design.* London: Orbis, 1985.

———. *Columbus: The Great Adventure: His Life, His Times, ans His Voyages.* Trans. Luciano F. Farina and Marc A. Beckwith. New York: Orion Books, 1991.

Thacher, John Boyd. *Christopher Columbus, His Life, His Work, His Remains.* 3 Vols. New York: AMS Press, Inc. 1967.

Watts, Pauline Moffitt. "Prophecy and Discovery: On the Spiritual Origins of Christopher Columbus's 'Enterprise of the Indies.'" *American Historical Review* (1985) 90:73-102.

West, Delno C. "Writings: Marginalia." *The Christopher Columbus Encyclopedia.* 2 Vols. Ed. Silvio A. Bedini. New York: Simon & Schuster, 1992. 2:746-48.

———. and August Kling. *The Libro de las profecías of Christopher Columbus.* Gainesville: University of Florida Press, 1991.

———. and Jean M. West. *Christopher Columbus: The Great Adventure and How We Know about It*. New York: Atheneum, 1991.

Whitney, Orson F. *The Life of Heber C. Kimball*. Salt Lake City: Bookcraft, Inc., 1978.

Widtsoe, John A. *Man and the Dragon*. Salt Lake City: Bookcraft, 1945.

Index

— A —

Abraham, 2, 4
Adam, 2
Adams, John, 4
Admiral of the Open Sea (book), xii
Adriatic Sea, 13
Aegean Sea, 13, 17
Africa, 14, 20, 24, 27
Age of Discovery, vii, 5
Agosto, Aldo, on CC education, 11
American natives, 46–48; aggression of, 67–68; baptism in Spain, 53–54; CC desired to convert to Christianity, 58
Americas, xi, 3, 4, 32
Antillia Island, 27
Asia, 20, 27
Asserto Document, 8
Atlantic Ocean, 1, 19, 21, 24, 27
Azores Islands, 41, 51

— B —

Barcelona, Spain, 53
Beaujeu, Anne de, 35
Bedini, Silvio A., on CC signature, 10
Belén, 67–68
Benson, Ezra Taft: on CC, 2; on Wilford Woodruff's work for the dead, 72
Black Sea, 14
Bobadilla, Francisco de, 62
Book of Mormon, prophecy fulfilled, v, 56
Book of Prophecies (book), xi, 62, 67
Brigham, Kay, *Christopher Columbus's Book of Prophecies*, 64
Buil Bernardo, 58

— C —

Cadiz, Spain, 58
Caffa, 13–14
Canary Islands, viii, 41, 58
Cannon, George Q.: on CC, 2; on forerunners to restoration of gospel, 4
Cape of Good Hope, 35
Cape St. Vincent, 20
Capitana (ship), 68
Castile, 8, 69
Charles VIII (French king), 35
Cheesman, Paul: *The World of the Book of Mormon*, 47; on bearded white God legend, 47–48
China, 26, 27
Chios, 17, 24
Christianity, CC's interest in spreading of, 30–33, 56, 65
Christopher Columbus's Book of Prophecies (book), 64
Church of Jesus Christ, restoration of, 71
Colón, Diego, 54
Columbus, Bartholomew (brother of CC), 10, 35, 60, 61, 67–68
Columbus, Bianchinetta (sister of CC), 11
Columbus, Christopher (herein referred to as CC):

Beliefs and Opinions

American natives, 46, 48; Enterprise of the Indies, 65; CC fulfilled prophecy, v, 64; God's direction in CC's life, 3, 27, 41, 50; CC an instrument in God's hand, 30; lifespan of earth, 30–31, 65; miracle of first voyage, 43; prophecies of Isaiah, 65–66; sailing experience, 15; spirituality, 66–67; spreading of Christianity, 32

Personal Characteristics

Character, 12; description, 12; desired to spread Christianity, xi, 30–33, 56; faith in God, ix, 50, 51; fulfilled prophecy, xi, 56, 66; instrument in God's hands, ix, 4, 32, 33, 71; knew scriptures, 14, 25, 63–65, 66; mistakes about geography and navigation, vii–viii; motivated to serve God, 30, 48; obsessed with conversion of all the world, 31; quoted scriptures, 63–65; religious attitude, 12–13; signature, 10; significance of name, 8–10

Personal History and Experiences

Birth, 1, 7–8; childhood, 10–13; family, 10–11; education, 11–12, 24–28, 63; early years at sea, 15–17;

presence of Moroni, 3; skillful sailor, 15; letters to Spanish crown, 15, 64–66; sea merchant and sailing experiences, 17, 21, 24; moves to Portugal, 19, 34; attacked by French war fleet, 20; intervention of God, 20, 37; map maker, 20; employed by DiNegro family, 21; marriage, 21–24; moves to Madeira Islands, 23–24; birth of son, Diego, 24; formulates plan of sailing west to India, 24–28; correspondence with Toscanelli, 26–27, 31; presents plan to Portuguese crown, 27–28; moves to Spain, 28–29, 35, 36; letter to Amerigo Vespucci, 30; influenced by *Imago Mundi*, 30–31; search for sponsor, 33–37; presents plan to Spanish crown, 33–34, 35, 36; second son born, Ferdinand, 34; affair with Beatriz Enriquez de Arana, 34–35; plan accepted by Spain, 37; first voyage, xi, 3, 39–52; honored by Spanish court, 45, 53; egg incident, 54–55; second voyage, 52, 53, 55–59; third voyage, 60–62; dismissed as governor of New World, 63; wrote *Book of Prophecies*, xii, 62, 67; wrote *Raccolta di documenti e studi publicati della R. Commissione Colombiana per quarto centenario della scoperta dell' America*, 63–64; fourth voyage, 67–69; death, 69; temple work done by Wilford Woodruff, 72
Columbus, Diego (son of CC), 24, 28, 29, 36
Columbus, Domenico (father of CC), 10, 11
Columbus, Felipa Perestrello e Moniz (wife of CC), 21–24, 28
Columbus, Ferdinand (son of CC), 15, 34, 67; on CC education, 11; on CC in sea battle, 20; on courtship of CC and Felipa, 23; on CC fulfillment of prophecy, 66; on definition of CC name, 9; on God's intervention in CC's life, 20; *The Life of the Admiral Christopher Columbus*, xii
Columbus, Giacomo (Diego) (brother of CC), 10, 59
Columbus, Giovanni Pellegrino (brother of CC), 10
Columbus, Susanna Fontanarossa (mother of CC), 10
Columbus Library, 25
Constantinople, 13
Convento dos Santos, 23
Costa Rica, 67
Cubs, 47, 59

—D—

d'Ailly Pierre, 27, 65; *Imago Mundi*, 25–26, 30
Declaration of Independence signers, 71–72
Description of the World (book), 25, 26, 30
Diario of Christopher Columbus's First Voyage to America, The, 1492–1493 (book), xii
Dias, Bartholomew, 35
DiNegro family, 19, 21
Dominica, 58
Dominican Republic, 49, 59
Dunn, Oliver, *The Diario of Christopher Columbus's First Voyage to America, 1492–1493*, xii

—E—

Earth: fable of flatness, 28; lifespan, 30–31, 65; sphere, i
Egg incident, 54–55
England, 8, 19, 35
Enriquez de Arana, Beatriz, vii, 34–35
Enterprise of the Indies, 24, 27, 30, 31, 33, 36, 37, 65, 66
Eugenius (pope), 31
Europe, xi, 14, 27

—F—

Ferdinand (Spanish monarch), 7, 32, 34, 35, 52, 53; desire to convert natives to Christianity, 58; letters from CC, 15, 64–66; CC plan presented to, 33–34
First Presidency, statement on role played by great people of other faiths, 33
First voyage, xi, 3, 39–46; CC guided by Spirit, xi, 2, 14, 41; CC credits God with success, 41; miracle, 43; course altered twice, 43–45; crew threatened mutiny, 43–44; first sight of land, 45; explored Caribbean, 46–49; landed at Cuba, 47; landed at Hispaniola, 48; Christmas in Americas, 49; homeward voyage, 50–52; returned by different route, 50; storm, 51
Flanders, 19
Florida, 61
Founding Fathers, 4, 71
Fourth voyage, 67–69; discovery of South

American lands, 67; crew killed by natives, 67–68; CC called to repentance, 68–69; return to Spain, 69
France, 8
Franklin, Benjamin, 4, 72
Funchal, 24
Fust, Johann, 14

— G —

Gallo, Antonio, on CC sailing at early age, 15
Garr, Arnold K., ix
Genoa, Italy, 2, 8, 15
Germany, 8
God: credited by CC for inspiration, 27, 41; CC instrument in hands of, ix, 4, 32, 33, 71; CC motivated to serve, 48; guided CC, 3, 41, 44; legend of bearded white god, 47–48
Gold, 56, 59, 60, 67
Gold Coast, 24
Gonzales de Mendoza, Pedro, 54
Goodrich, Charles, vii
Gospel, restoration of, xi, 3–5
Granada, 34, 36
Grand Khan of Cathay, 26, 31, 32
Greece, 8
Guadeloupe, 58
Gulf of Paria, 61
Gutenberg Bible, 14
Gutenberg, Johann, 14
Gutiérrez, Pedro, 45

— H —

Haiti, 49
Henry the Navigator, 20
Henry VII (English king), 35
Hispaniola, 48–49, 55, 56, 58, 59, 61
Historia del Mondo Nuovo (book), 55
Historia Rerum (book), 25
Holy Ghost, influenced CC, xi, 14
Honduras, 67
Huelva, Spain, 51
Hyde, Orson, on CC, 3

— I —

Iceland, 21
Imago Mundi (book), 25–26, 30
Indian Ocean, 67
Irving, Washington, vii; on egg incident, 55
Isabela (settlement), 59, 60
Isabella (Spanish monarch), 7, 32, 33, 35, 53; accepts CC plan, 37; CC appeared before, 36, 52; desire to convert natives to Christianity, 58; letter from CC, 15, 64–66; plan presented to, 33–34
Isaiah, prophecies of, 65–66

— J —

Jamaica, 59
Japan, viii, 26
Jefferson, Thomas, 4
Jerusalem, ix, 65
Jesus Christ, second coming, ix, 31
John II (Portuguese king), 27–28, 34
Juan, Infante Don, 53

— K —

Kelly, James, Jr., *The Diario of Christopher Columbus's First Voyage to America, 1492–1493,* xii
Kimball, Spencer W., 33; on CC, 2
Kling, August, *The Libro de las Profecías of Christopher Columbus*, xii, 64

— L —

La Rábida, 29, 36
Las Casas, Bartolomé de: on altered course during first voyage, 43; on CC as sailor, 24; on CC description, 12; on CC religiosity, 12–13; on God's help with CC, 44; on governing Hispaniola colonists, 59; on presented plan to Spain, 35; on spreading Christianity, 32; on tobacco, 48
Lehi, descendants reintroduced to Christianity, 32
Libro de las Profecías of Christopher Columbus, The (book), *vi, 64*
Life of the Admiral Christopher Columbus, The, xiii
Lisbon, Portugal, 20, 27, 29
Lisbon River, 51
Lollis, Cesare de, 63
Long Island, (Caribbean), 44

— M —

Madeira Islands, 21–23
Marchena, Antonio de, 29
Mariagalante (ship), 58
Marseilles, France, 17, 24

Martinique, 67
Martyr, Peter, 49
McCallister, John D. T., St. George Temple work for the dead, 72
Medea, 66
Mediterranean Sea, 17, 19, 24
Miracle, on first voyage, 43
Moniz, Isabel, 23
Moors, war with Spain in Granada, 34, 36
Morison, Samuel Eliot: *Admiral of the Ocean Sea*, xii; on altered course during first voyage, 43; on CC description, 12; on CC education, 11
Moroni, 3
Mutiny, 43–44

— N —

Navidad (fort and harbor), 49, 58–59
Nephi, 1; vision of, 56
Nevis, 58
New World. *See* Americas
Nibley, Hugh, on CC and first sight of land, 45–46
Nicaragua, 67
Niña (ship), 50, 51, 55
Nowell, Charles, on CC, vii
Nunn, George E.: on CC, 39; on CC choice of routes, 41, 50

— O —

Oceanic navigation, 20
Old World. *See* Europe
Ortiz, Diogo, 28
Otranto, Italy, 13
Ottoman Empire, 13–14
Ovando, Niicolás de, 62
Oviedo, 54; on CC, 12

— P —

Palestine, 14
Palos, Spain, 29, 41, 51
Panama, 67
Paverano, 11
Pavia University, 11
Perestrello, Bartholomew, 21–23
Perestrello, Bartholomew (son), 23
Pérez, Juan, 29
Petersen, Mark E.: on CC, 2; on destiny of America, 4; on restoration of gospel, 5
Phillips, Carla Rahn, 20
Phillips, William D., Jr., 20
Pinta (ship), 45, 50, 52, 55
Pinzón, Martin, 45
Pipino, Francesco, 30
Pius II (pope), *Historia Rerum*, 25
Pollution, viii
Polo, Marco, 27; *Description of the World*, 25, 26, 30
Ponce de Léon, Juan, first known European to set foot in future U.S.A., 61
Porto Santo, 23, 24
Portugal, 8, 19
Portuguese, preeminent sailors and explorers, 20
Premortality, 71
Printing press, 14
Prophecy, xi; CC belief of fulfilling, 64; in Book of Mormon
fulfilled by CC, xi, 14, 56
Prophets, on CC, xi, 1–3
Protestant Reformation, 14
Puerto Plata, 59
Puerto Rico, 58

— R —

Raccolta di documenti e studi publicati della R. Commissione Colombiana per quarto centenario della scoperta dell' America, 63–64
Restoration of the Gospel. *See* Gospel, restoration of
Revolutionary War, 4
Roberts, Brigham H., on role played by great people of other faiths, 32–33
Robertson, William, vii
Roldán, Francisco, 61

— S —

Saint Augustine, 65
St. Croix, 58
St. George Temple, 71–72
St. Kitts, 58
Salt Lake Tabernacle, 2
San Salvador, 44, 45
Sánchez, Rodrigo, 45
Santa Clara de Moguer, 51
Santa Fe, Spain, 36, 37
Santa María (ship), 49, 55
Santa María de Guadalupe, 51
Santa María de la Cinta, 51
Santa María de Loreto, 51
Santangel, Luis de, 37
Santo Domingo, 60, 61

Savona, Italy, 17
Schöffer, Peter, 14
Scriptures: CC humbled by, 66; quoted by CC, 64–65; studied by CC, 14, 25, 63
Second voyage, 55–60; desire to spread Christianity, 56; partially fulfilled Book of Mormon prophecy, 56; search for gold, 56–58; explored Cuba, 59; unsuccessful governor, 59–60; consented to use of slavery in Caribbean, 59, return to Spain, 60
Seneca, *Medea*, 66
"Serpent's Mouth," 61
Seville, Spain, 25
Slavery, viii, 59
Smith, Joseph, 1; used analogy of egg incident, 55
Smith, Joseph F.: on CC, 2; on destiny of America, 4
Social injustice, viii
South America, 61
Spain, 28; war with Moors in Granada, 34, 36
Spinola family, 19
Strait of Gibraltar, 19
Syria, 14

—T—

Talavera, Hernando de, 34, 35
Thacher, John Boyd, on CC signature, 10
Third voyage, 60–62; CC set foot on South America, 61; CC accused of incompetent leadership, 61; CC returned to Spain in chains, 62; CC replaced as governor, 62
Tobacco, 48
Toscanelli, Paolo, 26–27, 31; on spreading Christianity, 31
Triana, Rodrigo de, 45
Trinidad, 61
Tunis, 17, 24

—U—

United States of America, 71
Unrighteous dominion, 60

—V—

Valladolid, Castile, 69
Venezuela, 61
Vespucci, Amerigo, 30
Villa, Pedro de, 51
Virgin Islands, 58
Vision, of Nephi, 56

—W—

Washington, George, 4, 72
Washington, Martha, 72
Wesley, John, 72
West, Delno C., *The Libro de las Profecías of Christopher Columbus*, xii, 64
Woodruff, Wilford, St. George Temple work for the dead, 71–72
World. *See* Earth
World of the Book of Mormon, The (book), 47

—Y—

Young, Brigham, on CC, 3
Young, Lucy Bigelow, St. George Temple work for the dead, 72